HOW TO BUILD A WEBSITE *FAST*
USING EXPRESSION WEB

**Works with any version
of Expression Web!**

*Save yourself time, money, and headaches by
using this manual to build your own websites.*

How To Build A Website Fast Using Expression Web

by Greg Keast

Kahala Press

P. O. Box 88563

Honolulu HI 96830

ISBN-13: 978-0-9845307-2-4

Library of Congress Control Number: 2011903865

"We live in a web of ideas,

a fabric of our own making."

Joseph Chilton Pearce

Table of Contents

SECTION 1
INTRODUCTION

Aloha and welcome to the world of website creation with Expression Web.

This is our first training manual for Expression Web, and it's written for absolute beginners. This manual will show you how to create a website as fast as possible without knowing a lot about Expression Web and the code behind it.

Ideally, this book is for someone who recently bought Expression Web or someone who doesn't know much about it but wants to build a site as quickly as possible.

It is important to note Expression Web is evolving quickly, and a new version seems to be coming out nearly every year. Software training manuals usually come out with a new edition each time another version of the software comes out; however, given that there are now four versions of Expression Web with a fifth in the works, this book was written to apply to any version of Expression Web. Differences are noted where relevant, but for the most part, the versions of Expression Web have more in common than they don't. In short, you should be able to use this book whether you have Expression Web 1, 2, 3, 4, or the upcoming 5.

And while every effort has been made to double and triple check the steps, if you happen to notice an error or discrepancy, please do not hesitate to contact us at admin@expressionweb.us. Our door is open, especially to constructive criticism.

With that said, let's talk for a moment about our theory of teaching and point out some additional resources we highly recommend.

The Teaching Method

First of all, this manual employs a learn-by-doing approach.

Learning about abstract concepts and terminology is important, but you will retain that information better, and it will mean more to you, after you jump right into the software and build a website.

The best analogy for this is how you would teach someone to fly a plane. You could attend ground school and read all about aerodynamics and the instrument panel and how everything works but all that knowledge is not helpful in the abstract. It is much easier to put that information to use after you have tried to fly a plane.

Of course, it can be an overwhelming feeling to sit in a plane and see all the dials and gauges and not know for sure what anything does, but if an instructor is walking you through the basics and showing you what to do, then you will have a context in which to put all the concepts and information you will learn later in ground school.

For building websites, it is the same thing. It might seem overwhelming when you are using Expression Web for the first time. There are a lot of tabs and folders and unfamiliar terminology but if you jump right in, it will eventually become more familiar and create a context in which to put your abstract knowledge. And unlike learning to fly a plane, if you do something that causes the program or computer to crash, it is no big deal.

Our strategy is simply this: *Show* you how to build a website as quickly as possible. You will not know and we don't expect you to know what everything is or does. We want you to understand the basic steps and how to get going. Once you can do that, then you can go back on your own and learn more about the theory behind everything and what every little button means and does. And so, when you get to that point and are ready to learn more about what everything means and does, we have a couple of resources we highly recommend. Please note these are only our recommendations, and you are under no obligation to use them if you don't want to.

Recommended Resources

One book we recommend as a resource is called *Head First HTML with CSS and XHTML.*

The book is well researched, a pleasure to read, and provides a lot of good information about the code behind Expression Web. And if you are going to create websites, then you will need to have at least a basic background knowledge of HTML, CSS, and XHTML. Understanding the code will help you to feel more comfortable with Expression Web and everything in the book applies directly to what underlies Expression Web. You can purchase the book by visiting us at expressionweb.us and clicking the Expression Web box on the home page.

If you are more of a visual learner, you can go to expressionweb.us and explore the Video Section. You will find many video tutorials on Expression Web and all of them are free. It might take you a while, but if you watch every video, you will learn a lot about Expression Web. And again, all the videos are free, so you can't really go wrong by visiting the site.

So while this training manual will show you how to get up and running on Expression Web, it is also recommended you explore additional resources and learn as much as you can about HTML, CSS, and JavaScript. These three languages are at the heart of website creation and taking the time "on the side" to learn them will pay off.

Now let's talk a little about Expression Web itself, what it is, and why we recommend using it.

What Is Expression Web?

Microsoft Expression Web is a software program for building and creating websites. The original program Microsoft created in 1996 was called Front Page but was revised and renamed Expression Web ten years later. The program can be purchased as part of the Expression Studio suite but can be purchased separately.

You might not be familiar with all this terminology, and we don't expect you to be, but Expression Web supports using multiple programming languages to build websites, including HTML, PHP, CSS, JavaScript, XML, and ASP.NET. Expression Web uses its own development server and allows you to preview your websites without having to upload them to a remote server. The first version of Expression Web was released on December 22, 2006, and the current version, Expression Web 4, came out in June 2010.

Why Expression Web?

In two words, economic reality—it doesn't cost a lot of money and has all the basic tools you need to professionally develop a website. In short, it has what you need to create a website, and it's cheap.

PRICE COMPARISONS AS OF MAY 2011 (amazon.com)

EXPRESSION WEB		DREAMWEAVER	
VERSION 4 (FULL)	$90	DREAMWEAVER CS5 (FULL)	$385
VERSION 4 (UPGRADE)	$48	DREAMWEAVER CS5 (UPGRADE)	$191
VERSION 3 (FULL)	$64	DREAMWEAVER CS4 (FULL)	$505
VERSION 3 (UPGRADE)	$49	DREAMWEAVER CS4 (UPGRADE)	n/a
VERSION 2 (FULL)	$115	DREAMWEAVER CS3 (FULL)	$947
VERSION 2 (UPGRADE)	$35	DREAMWEAVER CS3 (UPGRADE)	$199
VERSION 1 (FULL)	$44		

As of May 2011, the full version of Expression Web 4 sells for $90, and the upgrade is only $48. If you have an existing version of Expression Web 3, you might be able to upgrade to version 4 for free. Check with Microsoft for more details. And no doubt, Expression Web 5 is already in development and coming out in the next year or so.

By way of contrast, the main competitor to Expression Web is Adobe's Dreamweaver CS5, which retails for $385—nearly eight times the cost of Expression Web 1.

Why would you pay 8x more for something when it doesn't do 8x more stuff?

If you are looking to build your own website and don't have a lot of money to spend, it is hard to go wrong with the first edition of Expression Web, which, as of May 2011, sells for $44 on Amazon.com! When you consider the full version of Expression Web 1 initially had a retail price of $299, that's an incredible bargain. Although the interface has changed in Expression Web 3, you can still create the same websites in any version of Expression Web. And you can upgrade later if you feel like you are missing out on features.

You should also note that while it is possible to buy less expensive "academic" or "educational" versions of these programs, you generally cannot upgrade from them, so whichever academic version you get, then that's the one you will be stuck with unless you buy the next version at an educational rate or can afford the full retail version.

SECTION 2
THE PROCESS OF BUILDING A WEBSITE

Before building any website, it is important to understand the website construction process. This is critical because if you don't have a plan for the website and what it will look like, then what exactly are you going to build? It would be like saying you are going to build a house but don't know what it will look like or have any plans, so you go to a bare spot of land and start building, but eventually, you'd have to stop because you wouldn't know what you were trying to create.

Before you get into making a website, you need to have a clear vision of what the site will look like, how many pages it will be, how many pictures and graphics it will have, and what type of content. This way, once you start building the site, you will have something to build and model the site after.

If you try making a website without developing the layout and content first, you will be trying to develop the content at the same time you are trying to build the site and that usually turns into a major distraction.

You wouldn't start building a house out of the blue, would you? You could certainly try to, but without a plan and the proper permits, it wouldn't be long before you ran into major delays and trouble.

Even if you only have a rough sketch, a few photos, and a couple of paragraphs written out, then that is better than having nothing at all. We once tried to create a site without content, and it literally took ten times longer than it should have. Expression Web, although it is similar to a word processing program, is not a word processing program, and it is not the place where you want to be creating content. Create your content separately and bring it in as plain text or .txt files. This will save you a lot of time and grief and endless editing.

The Benefits Of Using Templates

In this manual, you will learn how to build a website using the templates that come with Expression Web. There are several reasons why it is recommended you build your first site using a template:

- There are many templates to choose from, and they can be customized to virtually any style or need.

- Building a site completely from scratch or without a template requires the highest level of knowledge and skill and when you are a beginner, it is better to start at a lower level first.

- There is no point in "rebuilding Rome." In other words, if a template site has everything you need and want, why would you start from scratch when you don't need to?

- Templates allow you to build a quality site in a short time with little background knowledge.

- Templates give you an immediate sense of satisfaction and inspire you to keep learning.

We don't see templates as taking the easiest road. Yes, they are prefabricated structures, but they can also take time to properly customize. And once you have some experience with building sites from templates, you can always go back and try building a site from scratch, but for now, you will have much greater success by using templates.

An Overview Of The Website Creation Process

To get started on building a website, get out a piece of paper and work your way through answering every one of the following questions. Take your time and think about what you want your site to be and to do. Try to visualize it in your mind's eye and imagine you are visiting the site for the very first time. What do you see? What do you expect to find? Is there anything about the site that would make you want to visit it again? The answers to these questions will form the blue print for your site. After you have answered these questions, then sketch a rough draft of how you visualize the site.

- STEP 1: Concept

  What is your idea? What is your vision for the website? How many pages will be needed?

  The first step in creating a website is getting clear on what your vision is for the website. There are over 182 million websites! How is yours different? What is the purpose of the site? If there are already websites similar to yours, how will yours be better or different? For the purposes of this training, we would recommend your site not have more than eight pages, but you can have more if you feel it is absolutely necessary.

- STEP 2: Content

  What is posted on the site? What type of material will be there? Where will the content come from—you or somebody else?

  Determining your content is the second critical step. On the net, *content is king* and keeping it fresh and original is of the utmost importance.

- STEP 3: Domain

  What is the name of your site? Will the name be totally original like Google or will it simply say what it is?

  A name is important from a marketing and professional standpoint. Picking the right name is a critical and often overlooked process. You should do an Internet search for your proposed name and see what comes up.

- STEP 4: Design

  What will the site look like? What colors? What layout?

  The design, in no small part, will be based on steps 1 to 3 and should look professional no matter what you decide the purpose is. A cheap-looking design will not instill confidence. Appearance matters. Spelling and grammar are equally important.

- STEP 5: Graphics

  What type of imagery do you want on your site? Will you have photos, art work, or logos?

  You don't need a lot of graphics, but the ones you do have should tie into your overall theme and concept. At the very least, they need to be professional and look sharp. You can either try your hand at making graphics using a program like Photoshop or Paint Shop Pro *or* you can hire someone to create graphics for you. Either way, it is never too early to start researching and looking around for the type of graphics, logos, and photos you might want to display on the site. For this training course, you will need to find at least one photo to place on the website you will be building.

- STEP 6: Functionality

  Will the website need to do anything? Is it a static or dynamic site? Will there be forms, surveys, or questionnaires?

  By this step, you should already have an idea about this, but it is important to remember that people like interactivity. There is nothing wrong with a website that gives out information, but you might want your site to do more than that. What do you want yours to do?

- STEP 7: Databases

  Will your website need a database? How complicated will it be?

  More than likely, if you want your website to do something, it will need a database. This is not a huge problem but is one that requires additional work and planning and a more advanced set of skills.

- STEP 8: Bells and Whistles

  Is there anything special you want your website to do? Slide shows, multi-media presentations, fancy drop-down boxes? Audio?

  These are items your website does not have to have but are sometimes nice to have.

- STEP 9: Hosting

  Which hosting service will you use? What type of server will you need: Linux or Windows? How much is your budget?

  Finding a host for your website is an important step and often complicated issue. There are many services available and each one has its pros and cons. Especially for a beginner, making an uninformed choice can have enormous implications later and become a source of frustration, wasted money, and lost time.

- STEP 10: Marketing

  How do you plan to market your site? What keywords will your site need and use?

  Even if you have the best website in the world, if you don't market it, how are people going to know to visit. If content is king, then marketing is queen! You should plan your site with marketing in mind and that includes advertising in the real world, not just the Internet.

- STEP 11: Maintenance

  Who will keep your site up and running? How do you plan on updating the content? How often? How much can be automated?

  Websites can be easy to get up and running but keeping them current and fresh takes time. You need to consider how your site will be maintained over time. What seems like a small commitment initially can become huge as time goes by.

Websites Built Using Expression Web And Templates

To give you some ideas about the types of sites you can create with templates, please visit the websites below. All of these sites were created in Expression Web, and all of them were built from templates that were later modified in several ways. Some have had custom backgrounds added, some have had professional photos and logos added, and others have had their navigation systems changed. Once you learn how to build from templates, you will not be limited to those that come with Expression Web and can branch out to a vast array of templates available on the Internet, some for free and some for a fee. The site, *freecsstemplates.org*, is one place where you can get quality templates for free and for a modest fee of $10 to the template's creator, you can remove any references or links to *freecsstemplates.org*. This way, the site will be legitimately perceived as yours, even though others can still download the template and build their own versions of it too.

Ponderlicious
ponderlicious.com

The Learning Project
home.thelearningproject.net

Fast Quiz
fastquiz.us

Expression Web
expressionweb.us

Pass The Smiles
passthesmiles.com

Kahala Press
kahalapress.net

Hawaii Film School
hifilmschool.com

SECTION 3
GETTING STARTED WITH EXPRESSION WEB

Now let's get going with Expression Web.

As of May 2011, there are four versions of Expression Web.

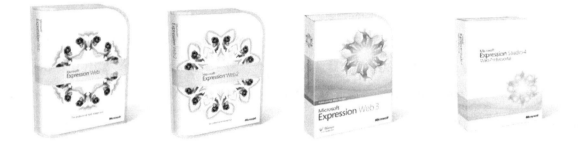

Take note we will be using screen shots from Expression Web 1 because all the versions are remarkably similar to it. The Expression Web 1 interface is virtually identical to Expression Web 2 while the Expression Web 3 interface is virtually identical to Expression Web 4; therefore, we will be using Expression Web 1 as the primary model for all the versions of Expression Web but will show screen shots from Expression Web 3 if and when it differs from Expression Web 1. Another way to say this is if you know how to use any version Expression Web, you can easily adjust and transfer your knowledge to any of the other versions. There are feature differences among them but not enough to justify writing separate manuals.

On the following page, take a moment to compare the interfaces on Expression Web 1 (top) and 3 (bottom). As you can see, Expression Web 3 sports a darker interface, but the general layout is identical to Expression 1. There is the common menu on top (FILE EDIT VIEW INSERT...ETC), two panels on the left, the primary workspace in the middle (in Split view), and two panels on the right. The primary difference is Expression Web 3 has more features than Expression Web 1, but you can still build a quality website with either version.

Microsoft has given version 3 a dark look, but it still shares the core functionalities with version 1 and most everything is in the same places. In fact, the templates we will be using to build your first website are identical in all the versions of Expression Web.

Sometimes when you open up Expression Web, it will open the last site you were working on or an untitled web page. If that happens, you can go to FILE, then CLICK either CLOSE or CLOSE SITE. In Expression Web 3 or 4, go to SITE and click CLOSE SITE.

Here is a clean shot of the Expression Web interface.

If your screen doesn't look like this, it means you haven't closed out the page or site that opened with the program. If the page is still there, go to FILE and click CLOSE or CLOSE SITE or go to SITE and click CLOSE. You want to start with a blank slate as shown in the image above.

Understanding Templates

The fastest and easiest way to build a website is to use one of the templates that comes with Expression Web. These websites are called templates, and they provide an excellent base from which to create an original and professional-looking site. In addition, under the software licensing agreement you consent to when you get Expression Web, you are free to modify and distribute them in any way you'd like. Let's take a closer look at them.

To get to the templates, follow these steps:

1. Go to the FILE tab (Note: If you are using Expression Web 3 or 4, you would go to the SITE tab, not the FILE tab to start.)

2. Select *New…*

3. Select *Website…*

4. Select *Templates* and you should see the screen on the next page.

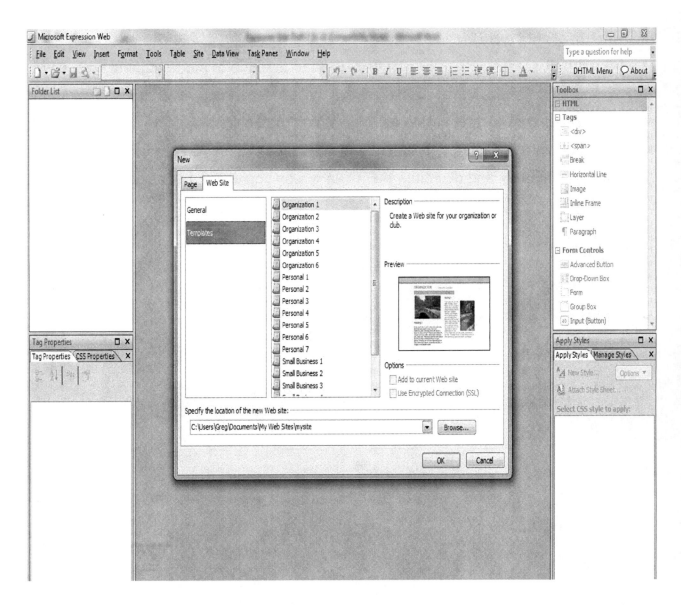

All versions of Expression Web come installed with website templates, and as you can see, they are divided into three categories: Organization, Personal, and Small Business. There are six organization, seven personal, and six business templates to choose from. You should note that just because they are categorized this way doesn't mean you have to use them the way they are grouped. If you want to use a "personal" website for your "business," that's fine. You should choose the template that best meets your needs and tastes. In total, this represents 19 templates you can choose from.

The beauty of the templates is the site's overall structure is fully laid out for you. All you have to do is go in and customize the content to meet your needs, and you've got your own site nearly ready to go.

Let's pick one to start with. We'll pick the template titled *Organization 1.*

Now notice where it says "Specify the location of the new Web site." This is the single location where you will place all the website's internal folders and files on your computer. It is also here where you name the main folder that houses all the website's folders and files.

In this case, let's call it "mysite" and that should be good enough for now. After you click OK, Expression Web creates a master or main folder where all your other folders will go to run the website, and at the same time, it will load the template into the main work area (or center panel of the program) of Expression Web, essentially creating all the website's files and folders right in front of you with one simple click of a button.

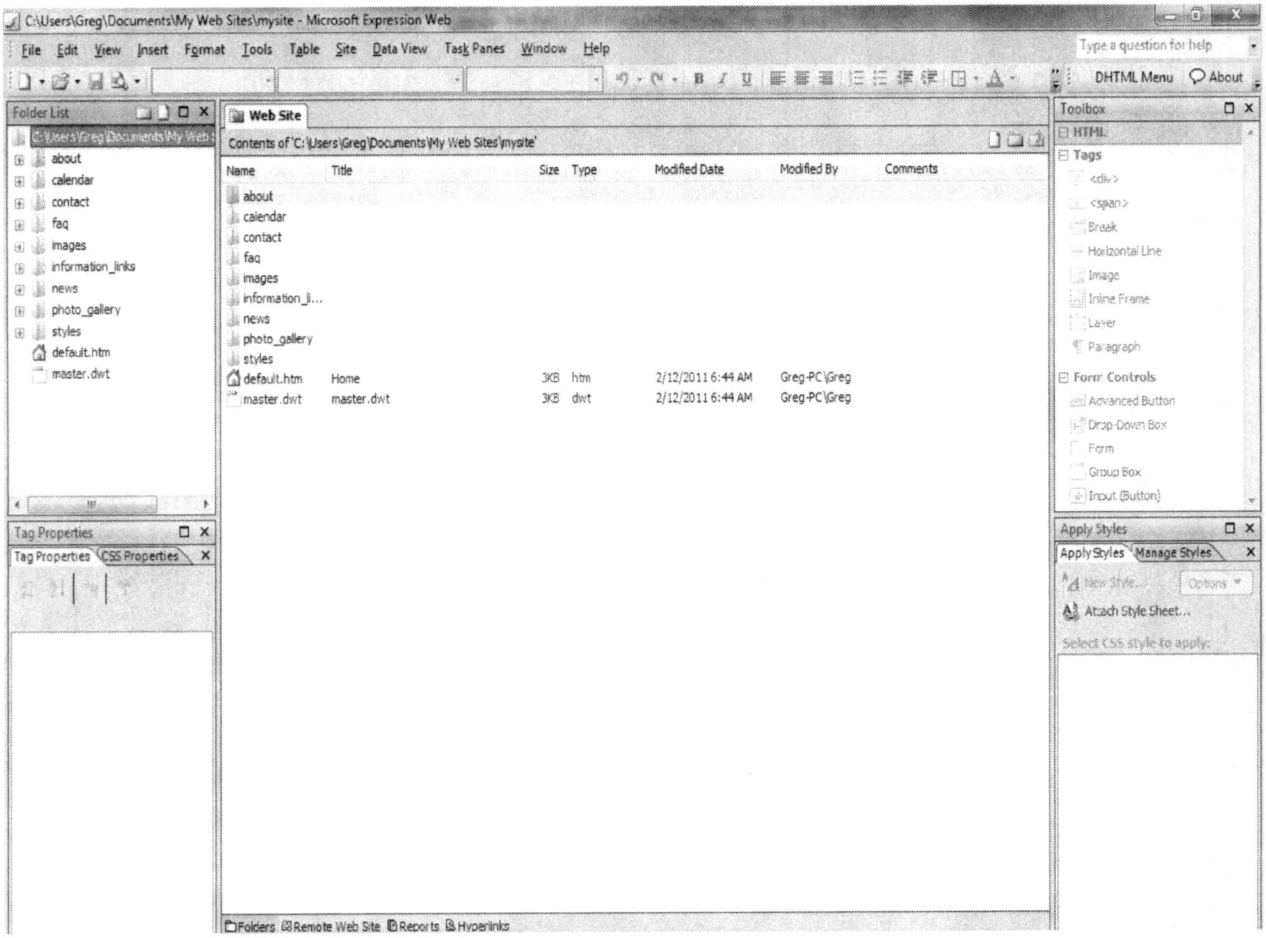

You should now see something that looks like the above screen. And believe it or not, this is a fully functioning website! Right now, you are viewing the website from the Folders view.

To see what the website looks like, double-click "default.htm" from either the Folder List or main work area. Please note on Expression Web 2, 3, and 4, the default home page extension is .html, not .htm. Practically speaking, there is no difference between .htm and .html; however, whichever extension you use should be consistent among your pages. Expression Web 1 defaults to extension .htm and that is why our examples end with .htm, not .html.

Your screen should look similar to this:

You should see the site in "Split" view, which shows the actual look or design of the site and the HTML code behind it. If the screen is not split, click the Split tab near the bottom left of the window. We will discuss these tabs more on a following page.

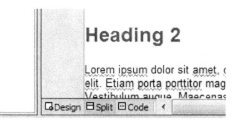

Now the site is created, let's go over a few things and click back on the Web Site tab near the top of the window. This will return us to the site's files and folders.

Starting in the Folder List, you can see there were nine folders created and two web pages. Notice the site's folders exist in two places, one in the Folder List and the other in the main work area window.

These folders are "subfolders" within your main "mysite" folder that we created earlier.

This template created an eight-page website, and each of the pages is housed within its corresponding folder name, so the About Me page is housed in the "about" folder; the Calendar page is housed in the "calendar" folder, and so on and so forth. The eight pages are:

Home   About   Calendar   Contact   FAQ   Information_Links   News   Photo Gallery

There are two additional folders that were created, and these are resource folders. The folder called "styles" contains *cascading style sheets* that control the look and layout of the site. The styles folder gives you three possible variations on your basic website theme. In this case, it defaults to style sheet 1, but it can be easily switched. A little later you will learn how easy it is to switch the style sheet, so you can play around and see which sheet or ".css file" you prefer.

The other resource folder is the "images" folder, and this folder contains all the images or graphics you will be using on your site. You don't have to keep your images in a folder but doing so helps keep things organized.

There were also two web pages created that are not housed in folders. The first is your default.htm page, which is the home page of the site, and the second, a master.dwt page, which is a template that makes it easy to make changes across all the pages in your website. Any site you build should have a dynamic web template. We will discuss this more later.

One thing you need to know is a website can only have *one home page*, and it is usually called your default or default.htm page. Often it's named default.html or sometimes index.html, but in our case, it's called default.htm. When you upload your website to a hosting account, it is programmed to look for and display the home page only.

Remember in Web Site view, if you double-click the default.htm page, it will bring the home page up on the screen. You should also note on the bottom of the page, there are three tabs labeled Design, Split, and Code. The tab you click will determine how the web page is displayed.

Heading 2

Lorem ipsum dolor sit amet, (
elit. Etiam porta porttitor mag
Vestibulum augue. Maecenas

Design Split Code ‹

If you click the "Design" tab, you will see the website as it should appear on the Internet. If you click "Split," you will see some of what the page will look like and some of the code behind the design. If you click "Code," you will only see the code and nothing else. If you are first learning Expression Web, it is probably best to keep the site either in the Design or Split view.

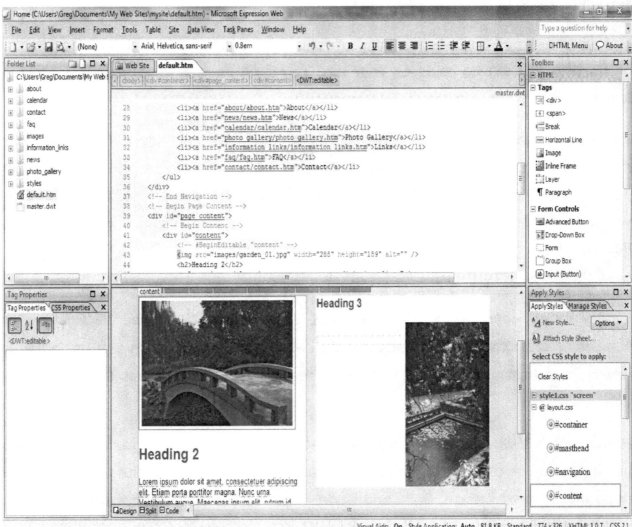

For now, double-click the default.htm file and click the Design view tab.

You should see a page that looks like this:

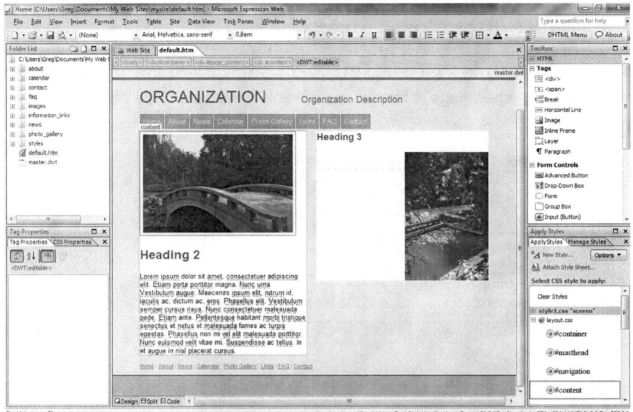

You can see that as you move your cursor around on the web page in some sections it is just a regular cursor and in others you get a red circle with a line through it.

In those sections where your cursor looks like a cursor, you are free to add content.

Go ahead and play around with typing in new content.

For instance, where it says "Heading 2," type in "My Home Page" or anything else you want. You can add any content you'd like. You can delete the content and add whatever you would like to appear on your home page. Remember, what you put on your home page is important because this is the first page people will see when they come to your website.

Now you should notice when you move your cursor into the navigation or masthead section, the cursor changes to a circle with a line through it. This means the content in those areas, at least from this page, is uneditable.

However, if you go to the Folder List (top left corner panel) and double click the master.dwt file, a new page is brought up, which is the master DWT page or Dynamic Web Template.

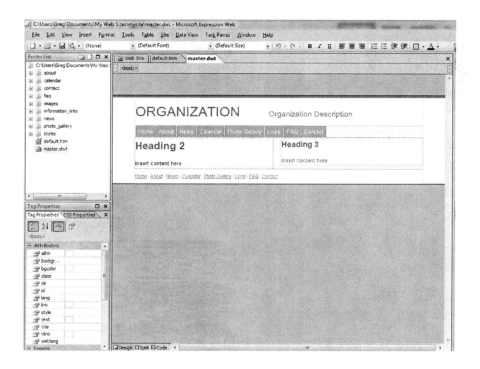

The dynamic web template allows you to share common elements or areas across all the web pages on your site. These common areas are generally the background, masthead or banner, navigation bar, section headings, and footers. These areas are usually things you want to be the same on all your pages, so there is no need for them to be recreated on each page. It is better if they are drawn from a template. This way, if you decide to change something on the navigation menu, you don't have to change it on all eight pages. You only need to change it on the dynamic web template.

On this particular website template, the masthead, navigation, and footer are all on the template. So let's play around with this a little.

Working from the master.dwt page, change the title of the masthead from "Organization" to "My Website" or some other name of your choosing. While you are at it, change the name of "Organization Description" to "This is my website" or something like that.

Now click Save on the top of the screen. You should also get in the habit of saving your work often. If you don't routinely save, you can end up losing hours worth of work.

You will notice after you hit Save, Expression Web prompts you by asking, "There are 8 files attached to 'master.dwt'. Would you like to update them now?"

When it says "8 files" what it is really saying is eight web pages are being fed information from this master web template, and it is getting ready to make the change you made on the template to all the eight pages. Click Yes.

So now it has made the change you made on the template and updated all eight pages.

Let's click back on the default.htm homepage and press F12 on your keyboard. What this will do is give you a preview of what the website will look like with the changes you made. You could also use preview by going to FILE on the top menu and clicking

Preview in Browser. Please note you cannot preview a .dwt page, only an htm or other web page. To exit Preview, press the Esc button on your keyboard.

Here's what the home page should like in a browser.

Notice the website address in the browser bar. It shows the exact location of the page on the computer and is the home page of the website, the default.htm page.

Now let's click the navigation bar and check out each page. As you can see this is a fully functioning, eight-page website. Congratulations! You have created and published your first website!

With this template site running in preview mode, this gives you a working example of how the website looks and performs. Click on each link on the menu and notice how the dynamic web template updated each page with the change you made.

Just remember any change you make on the dynamic web template will cut across and apply to all the pages on your site to which the template is attached.

To make this website our own, the only thing you need to do is customize the content and structure to meet your needs.

When we are dealing with templates and we want to customize them to our needs, we begin by looking at the existing pages on the template and comparing them to the pages we want. And in that regard, we will have one of the following three options:

Option 1: We can reuse pages.

Option 2: We can add pages.

Option 3: We can delete pages.

Let's start with first option.

Reusing Pages

For instance, let's say we are satisfied with seven of the eight pages, but let's say we don't want a Calendar page and would rather have a Blog page. When you rename and change an existing page, the content needs to be changed in six places. These are:

1) The web page folder

2) The web page file name

3) The web page title

4) The web page itself

5) The navigation menu

6) The footer

Let's go through each area now.

Renaming The Web Page Folder And Page File

Renaming the folder is fairly straightforward. In the Folder List, right click the Calendar folder, and a box will appear. Move down to where it says "Rename" and left click. Type in the name "Blog." Expression Web will automatically update the name and move the folder to the bottom of the list.

To rename a web page or .htm file itself, double-click the Blog folder and the calendar.htm file will appear beneath it. Once it does, highlight the calendar.htm file with one left click, then right click and another box will pop up.

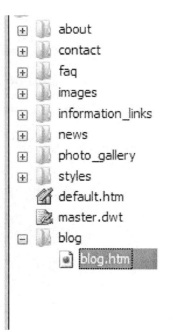

Mouse over to Rename, click that, then rename the page file to "blog.htm." Make sure you use the same extension that is in the original name. For instance, if the extension is .htm, use that. If the extension is .html, use that.

When you change the name on the page file, Expression Web will identify any hyperlinks to this page and ask you if you want to update these pages so "the hyperlinks will not be broken." Click Yes when prompted. Expression Web will automatically update the links with the new name.

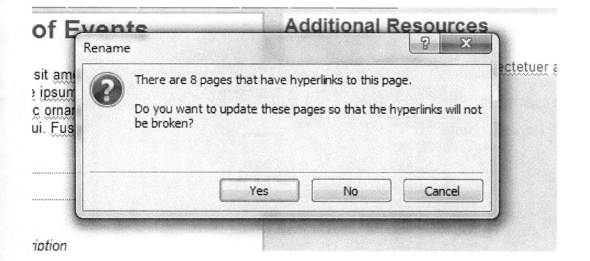

Renaming the Web Page Title

To change the page title as it will appear in a browser or on the web, make sure you are in the Design view and bring up the page in the main window by double clicking the blog.htm file in the Folder List. While in Design view, right click anywhere on the blog.htm page, and a box that looks like this should appear.

Depending where you click the page, your box might look a little different, but it should have an option that says "Page Properties…." If it does, click Page Properties, and it will bring up the Page Properties box.

In the field, second from the top, it says, "Title." Change the name from "Calendar of Events" to "Blog," then click OK. While you are at it, you can also fill in the Page Description and Keywords for your page. The keywords should be separated by commas.

You might notice after you do this, an asterisk appears on the web page tab in the main window. An asterisk there means the page is not saved.

Click on the Save icon in the tool bar to save. If any dialogue box appears, click that you want to save the most recent version of the page. If you saved the page correctly, the asterisk should go away.

Adding Page Content

Changing the content on the page is when you can begin to feel like you are building a site. (As we discussed in the earlier sections, it helps if you have your content already in mind. If you have to create the content while you are trying to build the site, it can waste a lot of time and become very distracting.) Make sure you are on the newly renamed blog.htm page in the Design view and delete where it says, "Calendar of Events" and type in "Blog" or whatever you want it to say. Working from within the web page itself is similar to working in a word processing program except it is mixed with HTML and other code. You just type in what you want and delete what you don't want. Again you should notice any change you make on the page will make the asterisk reappear, so be sure to click the Save icon or Ctrl + S before moving on.

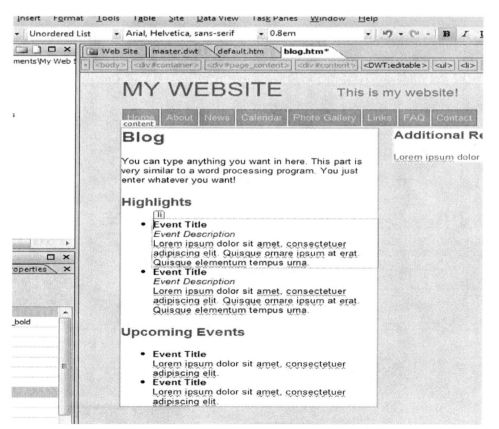

We are almost done but now need to make two final changes. For these last two steps, you will need to be working from the dynamic web template, so on the Folder List, double-click with your left button on the master.dwt file and it will bring up the template on the main screen. Now switch to the Split view and we will change the names and links on the navigation and footer. Your screen should look like this:

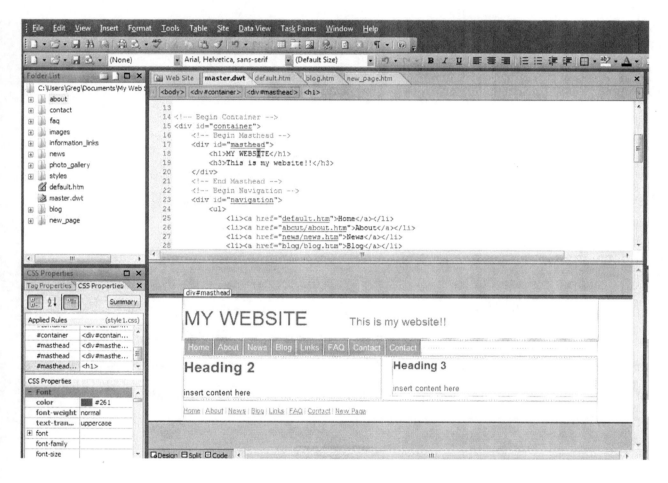

This can be a little tricky when you are first starting, so proceed slowly. Also remember if you make a mistake, you can always "Undo" what you did by clicking the Undo icon on the toolbar or clicking Undo from the Edit tab on top or pressing Ctrl + Z on your keyboard.

Renaming The Navigation Menu

To change the name on the navigation menu, find where it says "Calendar" in black font in the Code view.

```
     Web Site    default.htm    master.dwt    blog.htm
     <body>   <div#container>   <div#masthead>   <h3>
14   <!-- Begin Container -->
15   <div id="container">
16        <!-- Begin Masthead -->
17        <div id="masthead">
18             <h1>MY WEBSITE</h1>
19             <h3>This is my website!!!</h3>
20        </div>
21        <!-- End Masthead -->
22        <!-- Begin Navigation -->
23        <div id="navigation">
24             <ul>
25                  <li><a href="default.htm">Home</a></li>
26                  <li><a href="about/about.htm">About</a></li>
27                  <li><a href="news/news.htm">News</a></li>
28                  <li><a href="blog/blog.htm">Calendar</a></li>
29                  <li><a href="photo gallery/photo gallery.htm">Photo Gallery</a></li>
30                  <li><a href="information links/information links.htm">Links</a></li>
31                  <li><a href="faq/faq.htm">FAQ</a></li>
32                  <li><a href="contact/contact.htm">Contact</a></li>
33             </ul>
```

You can find this area quickly by placing your cursor on where it says "Calendar" on the navigation bar in the Design view. Wherever you place the cursor in the Design view it will appear in the corresponding place in the Code view and vice versus. Working from inside the Code view section, delete the word "Calendar" (that is in black font) and type in "Blog." Be sure to only delete the letters of the word and nothing else. Just as soon as you have made that change, save the page.

A dialogue box will tell you there are pages attached to the "master.dwt" and will ask if you want to update them now. Click Yes.

After you have done this, you should notice the name is now changed in the Design view. Changes you make in the Code view are not reflected in the Design view until you save the page.

Renaming The Footer

To change the name on the footer, it is the same process. Place your cursor on where it says "Calendar" in the footer. You should see the footer is up by the header. This happens because the template has no content in the center of the page and that causes the footer to rise. While still in Code view, look in the Footer section and find where it says "Calendar" in black font. Replace the word "Calendar" with the word "Blog."

Immediately save the page. The change should cut across all the pages.

At this time, make sure *all* of your pages are saved. You can go to FILE on the main menu and scroll down to where it says, "Save All" or if you have Expression Web 3 or 4, you can click the icon that looks like many discs on top of one another, right before the Super Preview icon on the main toolbar.

You will know all the pages are saved when you don't see any asterisks.

Now pull up the default page by either clicking its tab in the main work area or by double clicking the default.htm (home page) in the Folder List. Once the page is on the screen, press F12 on your keyboard.

This should bring up a working version of the website on your computer. Click through all the pages and notice the changes you made to what is now called the Blog page.

All the pages should work, and you should be able to tab through them.

Adding Pages

Now let's say you not only like all the pages you have, but you would like to add an additional page to the site. Thanks to the dynamic web template, this is not a terribly complicated process.

Making A New Folder

On the Folder List, make sure your cursor is not on or in a folder, then left click the Folder icon. This will create a "New_Folder" in the list. Right click the "New_Folder" and rename it to "new_page" or whatever you'd like.

Making A New Page And Naming It

On the Folder List menu, right next to the Folder icon, click the New Page icon. When you scroll over the icons, a little window pops up that identifies what the icon is.

Once you click the New Page icon, it should create a new page within the "new_page" folder called "Untitled_1.htm." If, for some reason, it doesn't, drag the "Untitled_1" page into the "new_page" folder.

Now, if you double-click the "Untitled_1.htm" page, the page should pop up on the main work area as shown below:

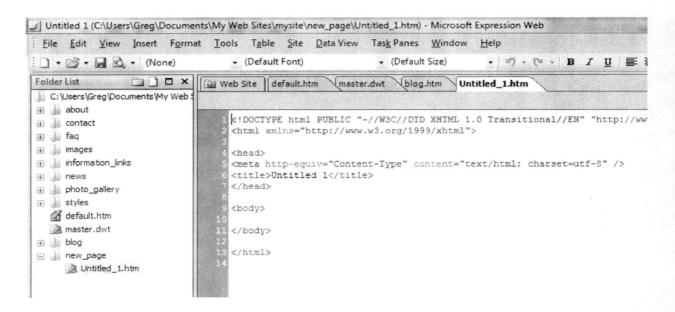

On the Folder List, click once on the icon where it says "Untitled_1.htm" and then right click the tab. It should bring up a pop-up box as shown below:

Click on "Rename" and rename the page to "new_page.htm" or whatever you want.

Notice after you change the name, the page name also changes in the main work area.

If the "new_page.htm" is not in the "new_page" folder, drag the page and drop it inside the "new_ page" folder.

Titling A New Page

Working from Design view in the main work area, right click the "new_page.htm" and go to Page Properties. In the Title field, replace "Untitled 1" with "New Page" or whatever name you'd like. Click OK, and then save the entire page.

Summarizing what we have done so far, we created a new folder, a new page, and titled it.

Formatting A New Page

Now we are going to format the entire page by attaching it to the dynamic web template. Go to the Format tab on the toolbar. Go to Dynamic Web Template, and then go to Attach Dynamic Web Template.

This will pull up a dialogue box with all the folders in the website. Scroll through the list until you find the "master.dwt" file.

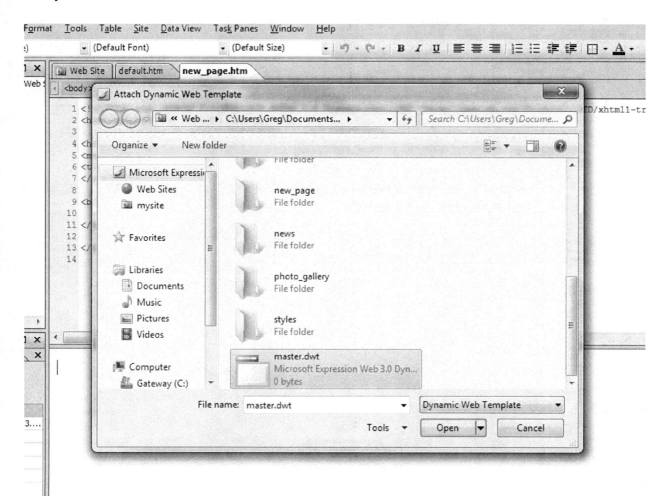

Highlight the master.dwt file by clicking it, then hit Open. Your New_Page should now be formatted in the same way all the other pages are. Click Save to save the entire page.

Updating The Navigation And Footer For The New Page

Now the only thing left to do is update the navigation bar and footer to link to this new page. For this step, we open the master.dwt page in the main work area by double clicking it in the Folder List, then choose Split view. Once in Split view, let's adjust the window so that 75% or so is in the Code view and the rest, around 25%, is in Design view. You resize the windows by dragging the border line between them.

Your window should look similar to this.

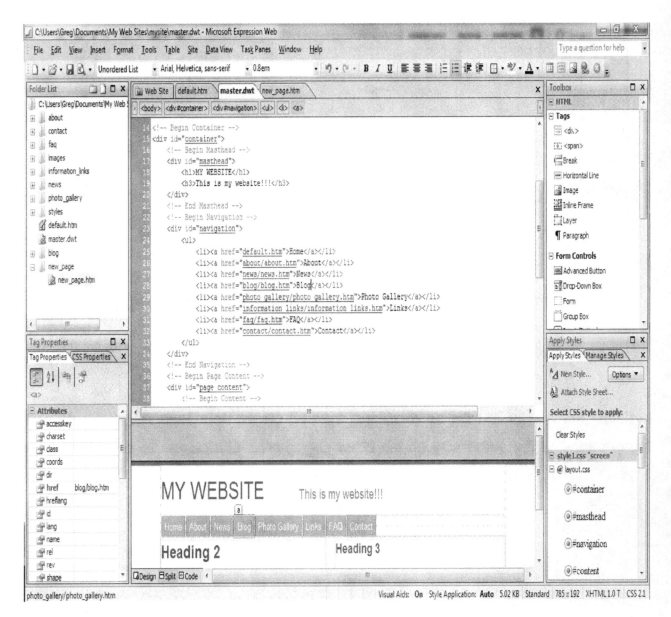

While in Code view, look for the section that starts with "Begin Navigation." When you are in the right area, you should see something like this:

Now highlight and copy the very last line of code in the unordered list (<ul>). The line of code is this:

<li><a href="contact/contact.htm">Contact</a></li>

Once you have copied this line of code, move your cursor outside that line of code and press Enter on the keyboard. This should create some space between the last line of code and the </ul> tag. It should look like this:

```
        <li><a href="photo gallery/photo gallery.htm">Photo Gal]
        <li><a href="information links/information links.htm">I
        <li><a href="faq/faq.htm">FAQ</a></li>
        <li><a href="contact/contact.htm">Contact</a></li>


    </ul>
</div>
<!-- End Navigation -->
```

Once your cursor is underneath the last line of code, right click and hit Paste.

If everything went correctly, you should have two lines of the same code.

```
<div id="navigation">
    <ul>
        <li><a href="default.htm">Home</a></li>
        <li><a href="about/about.htm">About</a></li>
        <li><a href="news/news.htm">News</a></li>
        <li><a href="blog/blog.htm">Blog</a></li>
        <li><a href="photo gallery/photo gallery.htm">Photo Gallery</a></li>
        <li><a href="information links/information links.htm">Links</a></li>
        <li><a href="faq/faq.htm">FAQ</a></li>
        <li><a href="contact/contact.htm">Contact</a></li>
        <li><a href="contact/contact.htm">Contact</a></li>
    </ul>
</div>
```

Now hit Save.

A dialogue box should pop up advising you that there are pages attached to the master.dwt file and asking if you want to update them. Click Yes.

Now watch what happens in the Design view.

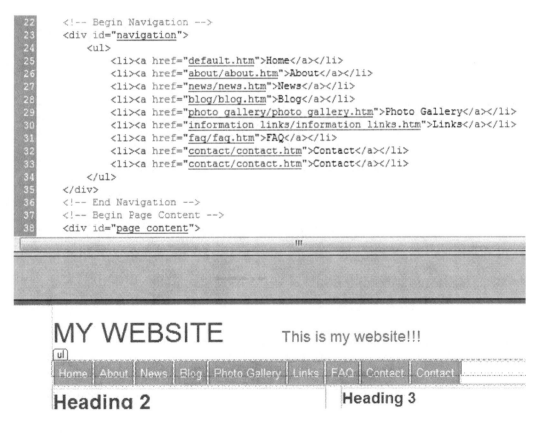

Note: If cutting and pasting isn't working for you, you can always duplicate the code by typing it while in the Code view section.

If all went well, you should notice you now have two Contact buttons on your Navigation menu as shown on page 52.

Now in the Code view, go to where it says Contact in black font in the second line of duplicated code you just created.

```
<div id="navigation">
    <ul>
        <li><a href="default.htm">Home</a></li>
        <li><a href="about/about.htm">About</a></li>
        <li><a href="news/news.htm">News</a></li>
        <li><a href="blog/blog.htm">Blog</a></li>
        <li><a href="photo gallery/photo gallery.htm">Photo Gallery</a></li>
        <li><a href="information links/information links.htm">Links</a></li>
        <li><a href="faq/faq.htm">FAQ</a></li>
        <li><a href="contact/contact.htm">Contact</a></li>
        <li><a href="contact/contact.htm">Contact</a></li>
    </ul>
</div>
```

And replace it with the words, "New Page."

```
<ul>
    <li><a href="default.htm">Home</a></li>
    <li><a href="about/about.htm">About</a></li>
    <li><a href="news/news.htm">News</a></li>
    <li><a href="blog/blog.htm">Blog</a></li>
    <li><a href="photo gallery/photo gallery.htm">Photo Gallery</a></li>
    <li><a href="information links/information links.htm">Links</a></li>
    <li><a href="faq/faq.htm">FAQ</a></li>
    <li><a href="contact/contact.htm">Contact</a></li>
    <li><a href="contact/contact.htm">New Page</a></li>
</ul>
```

Then save the page. It will ask you if you want to update the rest of the pages, so press Yes.

Now move your cursor into Design view area, highlight *all* and *only* the text where it says New Page on the navigation menu. You'll notice when you do that, it also highlights the words "New Page" in the Code view too. While still on the highlighted text "New Page" in Design view, right click and choose "Hyperlink Properties…."

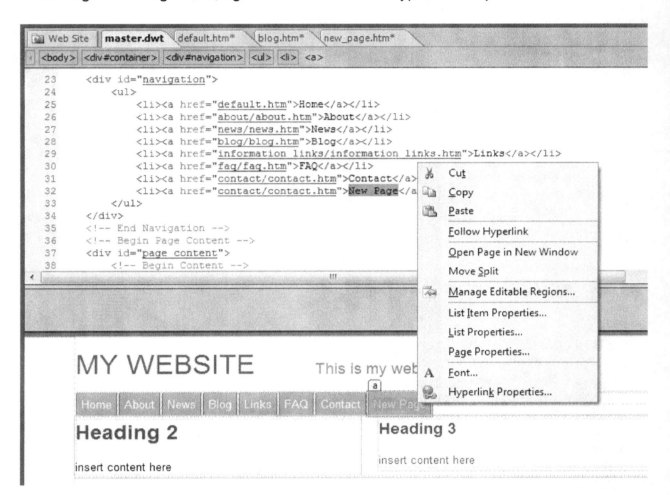

Note: It is very important to highlight only the letters and nothing else. If you highlight the brackets (< >) or any of the other code, the link might not work correctly. By working in Split view, you can work in the Design view, but reference the Code view to be sure your selection is exact. If you would like more precise control when selecting text or code, you can place your cursor in front of what you want to select, and then hold down the Shift Key on your keyboard while pressing the Arrow Key(s). This method will give you more control than using the mouse, especially in tight situations.

The Edit Hyperlink box will appear.

You are looking for the link to the "new_page" we just created, so double-click the folder "new page." Once you are in the folder, you should see the "new_page.htm" you made.

Left click that, then hit OK. If things went well, it should have created a new link from the New Page button on the menu bar to New Page itself.

Once that's done, save the entire page and click Yes to any page file updates.

Go back to the Code view. If everything worked correctly, you should see the hyperlink or "anchor tag" updated to the new page. It should look like this:

```
<li><a href="faq/faq.htm">FAQ</a></li>
<li><a href="contact/contact.htm">Contact</a></li>
<li><a href="new page/new page.htm">New Page</a></li>
```

If, for some reason, the link didn't update, then you can always type the link directly into the code as shown above.

Before we move on, let's check to make sure the link is working.

Double-click the "default.htm" page in the Folder List, and it should open the home page in the main window. Once the default page opens, press F12, and the website should open in a browser. Once it does, test all the buttons on the navigation menu. Hopefully, the new link is working, and you should be getting a basic understanding of page links.

Our final step is to add a "New Page" link to the footer following the same basic method we used for the top navigation bar.

First, toggle or click back to the dynamic web template in the main work area and find the Footer section in the Code view. It should look like this:

```
Web Site   master.dwt   default.htm   new_page.htm
<body>
47          <!-- #BeginEditable "sidebar" -->
48          <h3>Heading 3</h3>
49          <p>insert content here</p>
50          <!-- #EndEditable --></div>
51        <!-- End Sidebar --></div>
52      <!-- End Page Content -->
53      <!-- Begin Footer -->
54      <div id="footer">
55          <p><a href="default.htm">Home</a> | <a href="about/about.htm">About</a> |
56          <a href="news/news.htm">News</a> | <a href="calendar/calendar.htm">Calendar</a>
57          | <a href="photo gallery/photo gallery.htm">Photo Gallery</a> |
58          <a href="information links/information links.htm">Links</a> |
59          <a href="faq/faq.htm">FAQ</a> | <a href="contact/contact.htm">Contact</a></p>
60      </div>
61      <!-- End Footer --></div>
62  <!-- End Container -->
```

```
     <body>
47            <!-- #BeginEditable "sidebar" -->
48            <h3>Heading 3</h3>
49            <p>insert content here</p>
50            <!-- #EndEditable --></div>
51        <!-- End Sidebar --></div>
52      <!-- End Page Content -->
53      <!-- Begin Footer -->
54      <div id="footer">
55          <p><a href="default.htm">Home</a> | <a href="about/about.htm">About</a> |
56          <a href="news/news.htm">News</a> | <a href="calendar/calendar.htm">Calendar</a>
57          | <a href="photo gallery/photo gallery.htm">Photo Gallery</a> |
58          <a href="information links/information links.htm">Links</a> |
59          <a href="faq/faq.htm">FAQ</a> | <a href="contact/contact.htm">Contact</a></p>
60      </div>
61      <!-- End Footer --></div>
62 <!-- End Container -->
```

Now highlight, right click, and copy the very last line of code in the Footer section. The section of code you highlight and copy should look exactly like this:

| <a href="contact/contact.htm">Contact</a>

Once you have copied that line of code and while you are still in Code view, place your cursor between the last </a> and the </p> as shown below.

| <a href="contact/contact.htm">Contact</a>*place your cursor here*</p>

Once your cursor is in position between the </a> and </p> as shown above, right click and hit Paste. If everything went correctly, you should have two lines of code that look similar to this:

```
o gallery/photo gallery.htm">Photo Gallery</a> |
ation links/information links.htm">Links</a> |
q.htm">FAQ</a> | <a href="contact/contact.htm">Contact</a>| <a href="contact/contact.htm">Contact</a></p>
</div>
```

Now hit Save and click Yes to any updates, and watch what happens in the Design view.

```
59b gallery/photo gallery.htm">Photo Gallery</a> |
60ation links/information links.htm">Links</a> |
61g.htm">FAQ</a> | <a href="contact/contact.htm">Contact</a>| <a href="contact/contact.htm">Contact</a></p>
```

Use Ctrl+Click to follow a code

MY WEBSITE   This is my website!

| Home | About | News | Blog | Photo Gallery | Links | FAQ | Contact | New Page |

Heading 2

insert content here

Heading 3

insert content here

Home   About   News   Calendar   Photo Gallery   Links   FAQ   Contact   Contact

You should notice you now have two "Contact" links in the Footer section.

Now in the Code view, go to where it says "Contact" in black font in the duplicated line of code you created in the Footer section and replace it with the words, "New Page." By doing this you are renaming the second "Contact" name in the footer to "New Page." After you're done, save the page and say Yes to any updates.

Now in Design view, highlight *all* and *only* the text where it says "New Page" in the footer. You'll notice when you do that, it also highlights the words "New Page" in the Code view too. While still on the highlighted portion in Design view, right click and choose "Hyperlink Properties…."

The Edit Hyperlink box will appear. Double-click the folder "new page." Once inside that folder, you should see "new_page.htm." Left click that, then hit OK. If you did it correctly, it should have created a new link from the New Page link in the footer to New Page itself. Once you're done, save the page, say Yes to any updates, and make sure ALL the pages are saved, that is, be sure you don't see any asterisks next to any of the page tabs in the main work area.

Let's check again to make sure the links are all working.

Double-click the default.htm page in the Folder List, and it should open the home page in the main work area. Once the default page opens, press F12, and the website should open in your browser. Once it does, check to make sure all the buttons on the navigation menu and links in the footer are working properly.

Your updated website should look comparable to this.

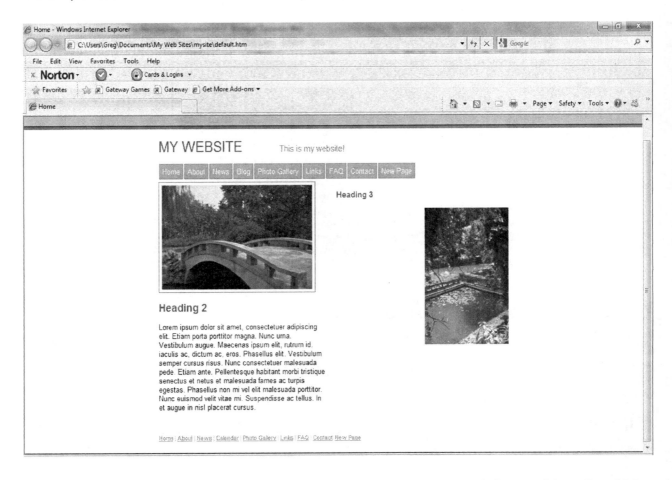

Notice the addition of the New Page in the navigation bar and footer. You should be able to click each link on the navigation bar and footer and be taken to the correct page. If one of the pages didn't update correctly, then delete that page, create a new page with the exact same name in the exact same place, and reattach the dynamic web template.

We will be going over dynamic web templates again, so you can see how easy it is to create a brand new page and quickly format it. Whenever you need to delete and replace a damaged page, you have to be sure to keep it right where it was and rename it exactly as it was previously named. In addition, if cutting and pasting isn't working for you, you can always duplicate the code by directly typing it into the Code view section.

Deleting Pages

Now let's say you like the template but only need seven pages instead of eight, and so you need to delete a page. This is probably the easiest process of all because all you need to do is delete the links to the page from the navigation menu and footer and for all practical purposes, the page will be gone and inaccessible.

For this example, let's say you want to delete the Photo Gallery page. To do this, first navigate to the master.dwt page by double clicking it in the Folder List. It will then open in the main work area. Make sure you are in Split view with most of the screen showing the Code view.

Locate the Navigation Section in the Code view and locate this line of code:

`<li><a href="photo_gallery/photo_gallery.htm">Photo Gallery</a></li>`

Once you have found it, highlight it, right click, and delete it.

Next locate the Footer section in the code. It looks like this:

```
 Web Site   master.dwt   default.htm   blog.htm   new_page.htm
 <body>
49              <p>insert content here</p>
50              <!-- #EndEditable --></div>
51          <!-- End Sidebar --></div>
52      <!-- End Page Content -->
53      <!-- Begin Footer -->
54      <div id="footer">
55          <p><a href="default.htm">Home</a> | <a href="about/about.htm">About</a> |
56          <a href="news/news.htm">News</a> | <a href="blog/blog.htm">Blog</a> |
57          <a href="photo gallery/photo gallery.htm">Photo Gallery</a> |
58          <a href="information links/information links.htm">Links</a> |
59          <a href="faq/faq.htm">FAQ</a> | <a href="contact/contact.htm">Contact</a> |
60          <a href="new page/new page.htm">New Page</a>
61          </p>
62      </div>
63      <!-- End Footer --></div>
64  <!-- End Container -->
65  |
66  </body>
67
68  </html>
```

Locate this line of code:

`<a href="photo_gallery/photo_gallery.htm">Photo Gallery</a> |`

In case you are wondering, the vertical line after the </a> is not code, but ornamentation to add a sense of separation between the footer links. (This is a little secret, but you make it by pressing your Shift key and pressing the backward slash (\ ).

Once you have found the line of code, highlight it, right click, and choose Delete or press the Delete button on your keyboard. Press the Save icon on the toolbar, say Yes to any updates, and allow the pages to be updated.

Next navigate to your home page or the default.htm page by double clicking the default.htm page in the Folder List or clicking the default.htm tab in the work area.

Press F12 and see if the links are gone.

In this example, the pages still exist in the website and you can see them in the Folder List, but by deleting any references or links to them on the navigation bar and footer, they are essentially inaccessible and gone from view. You never know when you might need the pages again, so it is better to keep them around and delete the links to the page versus deleting the page all together. If you truly want the page gone, then highlight it in the Folder List, right click, and choose Delete or hit the Delete button on your keyboard, and it will be gone for good.

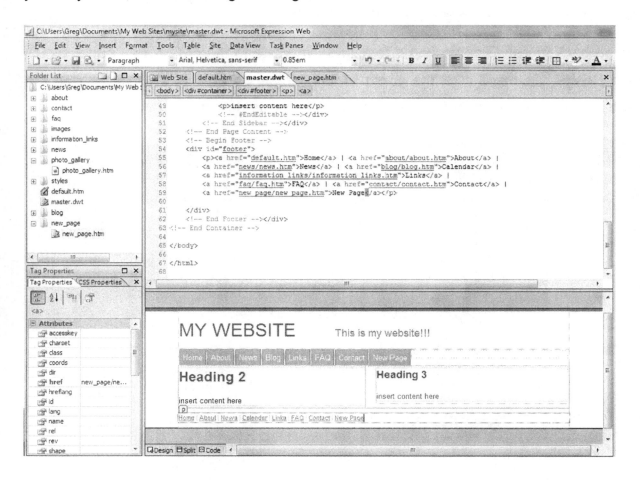

Now we have covered how to add, reuse, and delete pages, you can customize any template to meet your page requirements. Knowing how to add and delete pages is a basic skill you will endlessly use. And as mentioned earlier, if a page becomes corrupted for some reason, you can always recreate it by deleting it, then adding a new page, naming it the same as the deleted page and formatting it by attaching the master.dwt page.

Once you have all of your pages laid out and named, then all you need to do is add content in the form of text, graphics, and anything else you want including video and audio files.

Adding Images

Adding photos and videos to your site is not a complicated process, but before we do that, you have to have a photo or video to add. Any photo you have will do but make sure you know where it is located on your computer.

Let's go back to our *Organization 1* template. Navigate to the default.htm page, switch to the Design view and click the photo of the bridge. Be sure to click directly on the image and nowhere else. Your screen should look similar to this:

Once you've done that, look up at the top of the main work area, and you'll notice a little box is highlighted with the marker <img>. This is a representation of the image.

This area is often referred to as the breadcrumb trail and helps to show you where you are exactly in the code. In this case, seeing the <img> tag lit confirms you are on the image itself and only on the image and nothing else.

Now all you have to do is press Delete on your keyboard, and it will delete the image.

After you have deleted the image, click Insert on the main menu. Click on Picture and then click "From File…"

From here, a dialogue box will open, so you can navigate to where your photo is.

Once you find your photo, click Insert. After you do that, the Accessibility Properties box will pop up. Here you can enter a name for your image and a description. You should take a moment to enter the information.

After you click OK, the image will be inserted into your page.

Next you should save the page by clicking the Save icon. Once you do that, a "Save Embedded Files" box will open, and click OK again.

This will copy the photo image file into the website itself.

Click F12 to see what the photo looks like in your web browser. Press ESC to return to Expression Web.

If the photo is too large (as it is in our example) or too small, the image can be resized by right clicking the image and choosing Picture Properties.

Once you are in Picture Properties, click the Appearance tab, a dialogue box will open and give you options for many things including resizing.

You probably want to keep the box checked next to "Keep aspect ratio" and then adjust the width down to the 200-300 pixel range. Once you adjust the Width or Height, the other will adjust accordingly. Click OK when done, and you will be taken back to the page with the image resized to your specifications.

You can also adjust the image size by clicking the image, then dragging the borders to the size you want. There are many ways to resize your images. These are only two of them.

Generally speaking it is better to make sure your image is the right size before you import it into Expression Web. But if it is not the right size, there is no major harm in resizing it inside of Expression Web.

Also, as a general rule, pictures should be in a .jpg format and no more than 50 kilobytes or 50kB in size. Fifty kilobytes or 50kB is roughly 1/20th the size of 1 megabyte or 1 MB. Large picture files will slow down the load time of your page, and most people will leave your website if they have to wait too long for images to download.

If you want to keep all of your images together, you can drag your picture files in the Folder List and drop them in the images folder. Expression Web will automatically update the image link, so the photo will still appear on the page. Also note that since we added this image directly to the default.htm or home page, the image will only appear there. If we had put it in a common area on the dynamic web template, it would appear on all the pages.

Style Sheets

Let's look at one more thing before we close out this section. First let's go back to the master.dwt page or dynamic web template. Remember you can't preview the dynamic web template and can only preview from an .htm or web page.

Now let's take a closer look at the template in Split view with most of the screen showing code.

Looking through the code, scroll up to the top of the page until you find this line of code:

<link rel="stylesheet" type="text/css" title="CSS" href="styles/style1.css" media="screen" />

Depending on the version of Expression Web you are using and the template, it might look a little different or reference a different style sheet number, but there should only be one line of code like this in the template.

70

This line of code is telling us Style Sheet 1 or the file "style1.css" is controlling the look and layout of all the pages. The style sheet controls the fonts, colors, spacing, and basic layout of the web pages. Style sheets are like templates in that if you make a change on them, they will affect all the pages on the website. We won't go into too much detail about how they work, just know that one style sheet is controlling the basic look of the site.

If you click the *styles folder* in the Folder List, you will see it contains four style sheets, one for layout and three for style.

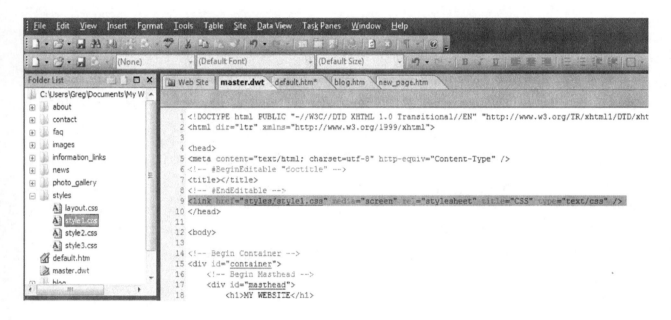

Templates differ on the number of style sheets they have and how they are numbered. For the Organization 1 template, we can see there are three style sheets available, and the current website is linking to Style Sheet 1 or style1.css.

Each style sheet has slightly different instructions for how all of the pages on the website look.

If you want to experiment to see if another style sheet better matches your tastes, all you have to do is change the link to the style sheet in the master.dwt template. To do this, go into the master.dwt page in the Code view and change the number of the style sheet from this *styles/style1.css* to *styles/style2.css*.

Or in long hand, change the code from this:

`<link rel="stylesheet" type="text/css" title="CSS" href="styles/style1.css" media="screen" />`

to this:

`<link rel="stylesheet" type="text/css" title="CSS" href="styles/style2.css" media="screen" />`

Please notice you only have to change ONE number to change the link to a completely different style sheet.

After you have made the change in the Code view on the master.dwt page, save your changes and say Yes to any updates.

To see if you like the new style sheet, navigate to the home page or default.htm and preview the page by pressing F12. You should notice changes, especially in the navigation bar. It is hard to fully appreciate the color differences in gray scale but from the screen shots below, you can observe differences between Style Sheet 1 on the left and Style Sheet 2 on the right.

If you are interested in learning more, you can also look at the code on the .css files in the Styles folder to study the exact differences in the styling instructions.

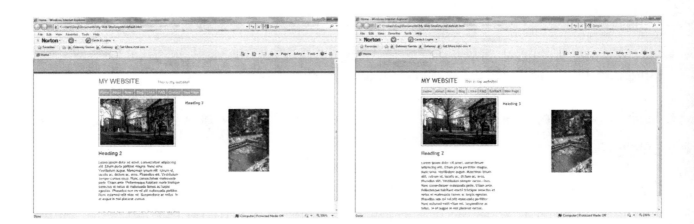

You can play around with the style sheets until you find the one you like the best. Expression Web gives you three different styles to try.

We have covered a fair amount of territory in this section. You have learned where to find the templates. You have learned how to add, delete, or rename pages and swap out photos. You have also learned how to change the style sheets for a different look and feel.

After that, it is simply a question of adding content and customizing it to meet your needs. It might take a while to get the site exactly how you like it, but the first site usually takes the longest. However, after you gain experience and confidence, it becomes easier and easier. The templates allow you to create a nice-looking website with minimal effort and without trying to build a site completely from scratch.

In the next section, we will go into dynamic web templates again and in more detail and hopefully get you more comfortable with using them. As you will see, dynamic web templates are very efficient and will save you a lot of time and effort in updating and maintaining a website.

SECTION 4
UNDERSTANDING DYNAMIC WEB TEMPLATES (.DWT)

We want to take some more time to talk about how dynamic web templates work in Expression Web. For you to be able to maintain a multiple page site efficiently and effectively, you should build it using a dynamic web template. If you don't, then any time you want to add a new page or make a change across all the pages, you will have to go into each page to make the change. By understanding how dynamic web templates work, you will be able to work smarter instead of harder.

To review, you can create a website by going into the template section and choosing any template you like. After that, all you have to do is customize the elements and content to match whatever it is you want. You can also swap photos and add audio and video. By using templates it is very easy to tailor a website to your original design and purposes. And if you change enough things, no one will ever know you even used a template.

The template sites are built using a dynamic web template and a style sheet. For now, we will only talk about the dynamic web template.

The dynamic web template allows you to share common elements among all the pages on your website. Generally, the common elements are the masthead or banner, the style sheet links themselves, the navigation bar, and the footer. You can also have photos and anything else you want to be the same across the pages. These common elements shouldn't change across the web pages, so there is no need for them to be recreated individually on each page.

Let's take a quick example.

To create a new website in Expression Web, open any one of the templates.

1. Go to the FILE tab in Expression Web 1 or 2 (left image below). Go to the SITE tab in Expression Web 3 or 4 (right image below).

2. Select *New…*

3. Select *Website…*in EW 1 or 2 OR *New Site…*in EW 3 or 4.

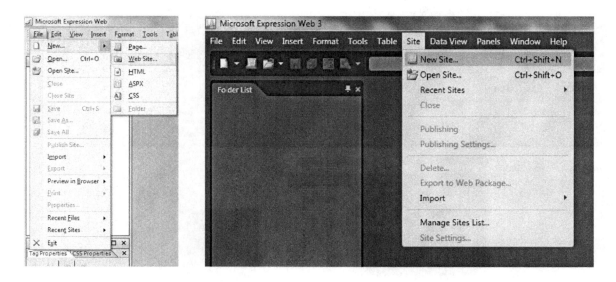

4. Select *Templates (which should bring up the following screen):*

5. Choose Organization 1 and click OK. The system will automatically name new sites you create by adding a number after the name, for example, "mysite1, mysite2, etc."

Now double-click the "default.htm" page in the Folder List and press F12 on the keyboard. The template site should open in your web browser. Take a look around the site for a moment. Click on the menu and look at each page. Notice it is a fully functioning eight-page website. It just needs customization!

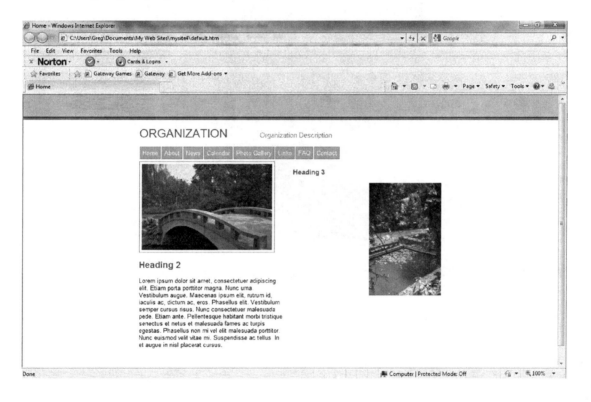

Now let's say you want to change the name "Contact" on the main navigation menu to "Getting Here." How would you do it?

All you have to do is change the name once on the template, and it will make the change on all the other pages.

Let's go through the process briefly.

Press Escape to exit the browser and get back into Expression Web.

In the Folder List, double-click the master.dwt file. This will open the file in the main window. With the window in Split view, move your cursor to where it says "Contact" in black font in the Code view.

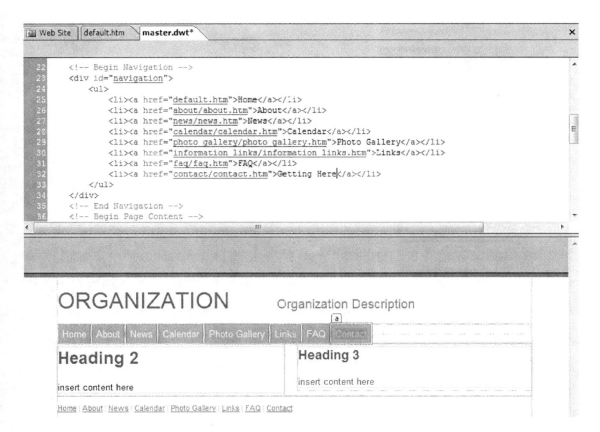

Now delete the text "Contact" and replace it with the words "Getting Here." (In the above example, for your reference, we've already changed it.) Then click Save. You will be asked if you want to update all the attached pages, so click Yes.

Now click over to the default.htm page and press F12. It will pull up the site in your web browser. (And remember you cannot preview the master.dwt page. If you press F12 when you are on the master.dwt, you will be asked to save the page and you don't want to do that. Plus, you will not be able to view the page. It will take a little while to remember you can't preview a dynamic web template page!)

Once the website is displayed in the browser, you can click all the pages and notice how the link Getting Here is now present on the navigation bar on all the pages.

The other thing to realize about the dynamic web template is it operates by feeding the content to the individual pages, and it doesn't continuously update or feed them again unless there is a change somewhere on the dynamic web template itself. You can think of the dynamic web template as an obsessive caterer who makes sure everyone is given the same meal and if the caterer is told of a menu change, it applies to everyone.

Changing The Style Sheet Link

It is important to note the dynamic web template is not the same as the style sheet. The dynamic web template provides the elements (for instance, the menu and list items), but the style sheets provide the instructions for how the elements will look. The dynamic web template supplies "the link" to the style sheets, but not the style instructions contained in the sheet.

To show you how this works, let's go back into the site we were just working with and change the style sheet link.

Go back into the dynamic web template, but switch to the Code view only. Now scroll up to the top of the page and look for a line of code that looks like this:

```
<link rel="stylesheet" type="text/css" title="CSS" href="styles/style1.css" media="screen" />
```

This is the link to the style sheet that controls the look and layout out of the pages.

If we change the 1 to 4 in the line of code *(that is, change "styles/style1.css" to "styles/style4.css")*, what do you think will happen?

Try it and see.

Working in the dynamic web template, change the 1 to a 4, then save the page and OK the updates. Now go to the home page (default.htm) and press F12 to preview.

What do you see?

Organization

Organization Description

- Home
- About
- News
- Calendar
- Photo Gallery
- Links
- FAQ
- Contact

Heading 2

Lorem ipsum dolor sit amet, consectetuer adipiscing elit. Etiam porta porttitor magna. Nunc urna. Vestibulum augue. Maecenas ipsum elit, rutrum id, iaculis ac, dictum ac, eros. Phasellus elit. Vestibulum semper cursus risus. Nunc consectetuer malesuada pede. Etiam ante. Pellentesque habitant morbi tristique senectus et netus et malesuada fames ac turpis egestas. Phasellus non mi vel elit malesuada porttitor. Nunc euismod velit vitae mi. Suspendisse ac tellus. In et augue in nisl placerat cursus.

You should see a page with all the elements on the page, but no style! The pictures are still there. The headings are still there. The text is still there. The navigation and footers are still there. And everything works!

But the site has no style because you killed the link to the style sheet. You killed the link because there is no style sheet 4! You told it to find something that doesn't exist, so the result was no style at all. You could have also deleted the entire line of code and that would have had the same effect. But we want to get you in the habit of changing the numbers, so you can practice attaching to the different style sheets that come with Expression Web.

So, in review, it is the dynamic template that feeds all the common elements and the link to the style sheet to all the individual pages.

If we go back into the dynamic web template and change the number back to 1 and save the page and OK the update, it will restore the style instructions to all the pages.

Another thing to understand about dynamic web templates is they are divided into editable and non-editable regions. All dynamic web templates must have at least one editable region.

If we go back into the home page, you will notice when you move your cursor to different parts of the page, it changes. If the cursor is in an editable region, the cursor appears as a regular cursor, and it will allow you to enter text or input data. If it is in a non-editable region, it will have the infamous circle with a line through it, and it will not allow you to input anything. You can only edit these sections from the dynamic web template.

You will also notice the editable regions also have a gold or yellow border around them. So when you are adding content to an individual page, the content you are adding can only be placed in an editable region and will only apply to that page. If the content you want to add should be on all the pages, then you should add it to the dynamic web template.

If you go to the dynamic web template itself, because it is the template, then you can go into the common areas and edit away. You can edit the common areas, the masthead, the menu items and the footer in the dynamic web template itself. But if you go to an individual page like the homepage, you can't. The common areas are not editable on the individual pages.

You should also know each page has its own editable regions, so you are free to add or delete content to those areas. If an area is editable, then it will let you add or delete data. If it doesn't, then it is a non-editable region and means you can only change it on the dynamic web template.

The question has come up: Can you have more than one dynamic web template per website?

And the answer is yes.

You can have as many dynamic web templates as you'd like. You can also attach or detach a dynamic web template to any page.

You would probably have more reasons to attach a dynamic web template than you would have to detach one but to familiarize yourself with how the templates work, we will try detaching one from a page to see what happens.

Attaching And Detaching A Dynamic Web Template

To attach or detach a dynamic web template, you go to Format on the main menu, then Dynamic Web Template, then choose either Attach Dynamic Web Template or Detach from Dynamic Web Template.

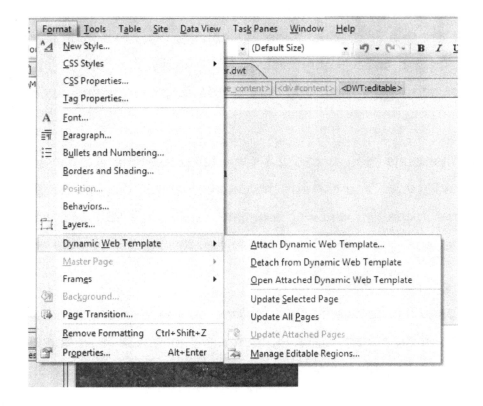

Once you detach a template from a page, you will notice the red circle with the line through it is gone, and you are free to edit anywhere on the page, including the masthead, navigation, and footers. The page is basically on its own but will still retain the original material fed to it by the template. It is for this reason you would not want to re-attach a template to a page you detached it from. Why?

Because the template would send all of its information to the page again, and you would have two sets of everything. On the page below, we detached, then reattached a dynamic web template. Can you see what happened? Now you can delete what the template brought in the second time it was reattached, but why bother? It is easier and cleaner to create a new page and reformat with a fresh template versus reattaching a detached template.

ORGANIZATION   Organization Description

Home | About | News | Calendar | Photo Gallery | Links | FAQ | Contact

Organization

Heading 3

insert content here

Organization Description

- Home
- About
- News
- Calendar
- Photo Gallery
- Links
- FAQ
- Contact

News

Lorem ipsum dolor sit amet, consectetuer adipiscing elit. Quisque ornare ipsum at erat. Quisque elementum tempus urna. Donec ornare fringilla erat. Phasellus gravida lectus vel dui. Fusce eget justo at odio posuere dignissim.

Top Stories

- **Event Title**
  Event Description
  Lorem ipsum dolor sit amet, consectetuer

To attach a dynamic web template, you create a new .htm page, then attach a dynamic web template through the Format menu. You should also know you can create a dynamic web template from scratch and use it to build pages but that is a more advanced topic.

Summary

Dynamic web templates allow you to share common areas across multiple web pages. They also provide the link to the styling sheet (.css file) the individual pages rely on for their look and layout. Dynamic web templates are divided into the editable and non-editable regions. The non-editable regions (the masthead, navigation bar, footer, etc.) can only be changed on the dynamic web template itself.

Every page has editable regions and this is where you add customized content that is unique to each page individually.

You can also create a dynamic web template from a blank html page, but you have to designate at least one editable region.

If you want more information about dynamic web templates, you can go to the Video section on expressionweb.us or go to Microsoft Expression Web online.

Again, if you try to create a website from scratch, you are going to find it is like being a white belt in karate and immediately signing up for a competition with black belts. Building a website from scratch requires the most knowledge and skill and when you are new to it, you are just not at that level yet. You will definitely get there with practice but when you are a beginner, it is much better to use a template.

Templates will allow you to create an original and highly customized website without all the headaches of trying to build a website from scratch, and once you get comfortable and confident with templates, you will naturally progress to a higher level of skill.

SECTION 5
UPLOADING TO A HOSTING SERVICE

In this section, we are going to explain how to upload multiple sites to a web hosting service or hosting account using Go Daddy. Web hosting services allow you to upload your site to their servers, and they take care of all the technical details and logistics of administering your site. You could try and run your own server, but generally, it is more cost effective to use a professional hosting service.

Why Go Daddy?

For the same reasons we like Expression Web—their service is affordable and gets the job done. In our opinion, Go Daddy seems to have some of the most reasonably priced and reliable services around. This is not to say Go Daddy is perfect, but it is to say that for the cost and value, they offer a good service at a fair price.

There are some "free hosting" services available, but quite frankly, they have a lot of issues associated with them. One such service is AngelFire, which is apparently affiliated with Lycos and Tripod, but when we last checked it out, the site was directing us to purchase services, even if we checked we wanted the "free" service. With the free services, you will not be able to have a free-standing domain name and more than likely, they will want to run "their ads" on "your site." So for now, the recommendation is to pay for the service and get what you need versus trying to get something for free that won't probably meet your long-term goals and needs.

So let's get started with the basics. The first thing is that to upload a website, you are going to need two things—a domain name *and* a hosting account.

Nearly everyone is familiar with what a domain name is but some of you might not have ever purchased one before. Buying your first domain name is exciting and if you're not careful, it might become addicting. Once you get one name, it is tempting to get others and others and before you know it, you could have all kinds of names, but not the time to build sites for all of them, so it is recommended you exercise restraint, take your time and carefully consider the name and how many names you can build sites for and maintain. You should also know once you register a name, you are stuck with it. You can't take it back or have it exchanged. It is yours until it expires, or you can sell it.

Also consider that generally the more time you put into developing a site, the more successful it will be. People are drawn to sites that have original and fresh content, so in order to keep a site worth visiting, it takes time and work. And you have to be honest with yourself and ask how much time you have to devote to maintaining any given site.

One reason it is easy to end up with a lot of domain names is that they are relatively affordable and cost less than a dollar a month, so some people have made it their business to buy hundreds of names in an effort to resell them. Some people call this practice "cybersquatting."

In terms of hosting accounts, there are a lot of hosting providers to choose from, and they all have their pros and cons. At this time, Go Daddy is the provider used for this book and as mentioned earlier, the primary reason for that is cost. However, this doesn't mean Go Daddy is not without flaws either. Let's talk about that right now.

One of the problems with Go Daddy is the sheer volume of things they are trying to sell you. There are so many things that it literally crowds their site. They are constantly trying to sell you add-ons that you can probably get by without. For instance, they often try to sell you on making your domain registration private, but the truth is if somebody wants to find out who you are, then they can probably figure it out.

On a side note, you should know that everyone's privacy is at risk and despite the wild success of sites like Facebook, you should probably take steps to control and manage how much personal information is out there on the Internet about you. For instance, if you are going to be publishing websites, then you should consider getting a post office box or business address, so when you register your domain name or do any other business online, you are not disclosing your private residence to the world.

Go Daddy also tries to get you to buy domains with the same base name, but different extensions. For instance, if you register the domain happytown.com, Go Daddy will try to get you to buy happytown.net, happytown.org, and happytown.biz. But the truth is when you are testing the water, one domain name with one extension should be sufficient. Go Daddy is almost always running promotions, so watch out for getting drawn in and buying more than you really need.

You need to stay focused and get only what you came for and that is a domain name and a hosting account. All the other stuff that Go Daddy is throwing at you, just ignore it. You can get it later if you must.

Hosting Account Prices And Plans

In terms of web hosting services, we compared Go Daddy with another popular service, Host Gator, and still found Go Daddy to be a slightly better deal.

PRICE COMPARISONS AS OF MARCH 2011
PER MONTH HOSTING COST BASED ON A 12-MONTH PURCHASE

GO DADDY		HOST GATOR	
Economy Plan	$3.99	Hatchling Plan	$5.56
Deluxe Plan	$6.99	Baby Plan	$7.96
Ultimate Plan	$9.99	Business Plan	$11.96
Domain Name	$11.99	Domain Name	$15

As of March 2011, Go Daddy offers three basic plans, which are shown below:

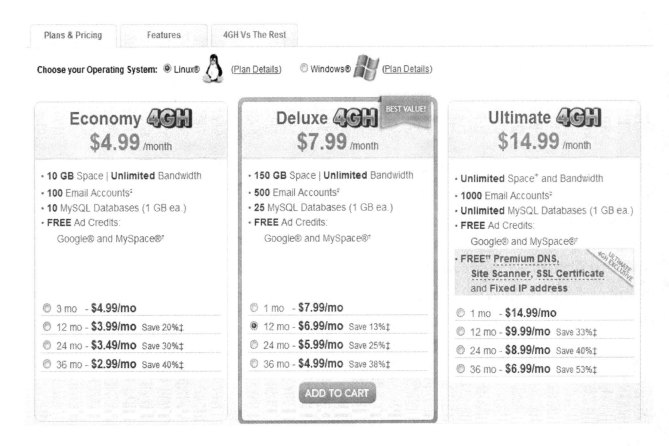

For our purposes, we don't have much interest in the Ultimate 4GH Plan. Especially if you are new to all this, it is doubtful you would need all the bandwidth and storage space it provides.

It is very tempting to go immediately with the Economy 4GH Plan because it is the lowest cost, but there is a huge downside to doing that. If you look at the features among the plans, there's one big difference among them, and it is shown on the next page.

	Economy 4GH	Deluxe 4GH	Ultimate 4GH
Monthly Fee. No Setup Fees.	$4.99	$7.99	$14.99
Min. Purchase Length	3 Months No Long-Term Contracts Required!	1 Month No Long-Term Contracts Required!	1 Month No Long-Term Contracts Required!
Discounts Available‡	12, 24, or 36 months	12, 24, or 36 months	12, 24, or 36 months
Disk Space	10 GB	150 GB	Unlimited
Monthly Data Transfer	Unlimited	Unlimited	Unlimited
FTP Users	50‡‡	50‡‡	50‡‡
Email Accounts			
Number of Addresses	100	500	1000
Total Email Storage	100 MB	500 MB	1 GB
Webmail	✓	✓	✓
"Light" Webmail w/PDA	✓	✓	✓
Greeting Cards - 290+ designs	✓	✓	✓
Forwarding	✓	✓	✓
Auto-Responder	✓	✓	✓
Catch-All Email Address	✓	✓	✓
Fraud, Virus & Spam Protection	✓	✓	✓
Sender ID	✓	✓	✓

	Economy 4GH	Deluxe 4GH	Ultimate 4GH
Auto-Responder	✓	✓	✓
Catch-All Email Address	✓	✓	✓
Fraud, Virus & Spam Protection	✓	✓	✓
Sender ID	✓	✓	✓
Email privacy & protection with 256-Bit Encryption	✓	✓	✓
Databases			
MySQL	10 x 1 GB	25 x 1 GB	Unlimited x 1 GB
Database Backup/Restore	✓	✓	✓
Direct Database Access	✓	✓	✓
Domains			
DNS Management	✓	✓	✓
Access without "www."	✓	✓	✓
External Domains	Unlimited	Unlimited	Unlimited
Subdomains	25	Unlimited	Unlimited
Multiple Web Sites	--	Unlimited**	Unlimited**
Alias Domains	Unlimited	Unlimited	Unlimited
General Features			
NEW! Assign an AccountExec	✓	✓	✓
SSH Access (Secure Shell)	✓	✓	✓
FTP over SSL (FTPS)	✓	✓	✓

If you look where it says "Domains" and under that "Multiple Web Sites," you will see that under the Economy 4GH Plan, you *cannot* host multiple websites. You can only have one website hosted and that is not good! However, under the Deluxe 4GH Plan, which is three dollars more per month, you can host *unlimited* websites on one hosting account.

Now think about that for a minute.

For only $3 more per month for the Deluxe Plan, you could host hundreds of websites. In addition, the longer your hosting contract is, the more of a price break you get. In other words, if you purchase your account for 12 months, you get 5% discount; if you purchase the account for 36 months, you get a 15% discount. Of course, always read the fine print on the site to be sure. These discounts are subject to change but offering discounts seems to be a long-standing practice of Go Daddy's.

Here is another money-saving tip:

Before you buy either a domain name or a web hosting plan, go to Google and type in "go daddy promo code" and see which sites come up. It should pull up a number of them.

On a recent attempt at doing this, the very first site that popped up was called *Fat Wallet*. And if you go to the site, you can see there are additional discounts available to you, some of them giving you a discount of up to 20% on the shared hosting accounts.

So if you can get a 15% discount by getting a 3-year plan and can get another 20% on checkout, then that's 35% off $7.99, which would be $5.20 per month for a hosting account that gives you the ability to host an unlimited number of sites. In fact, with the discounts applied, the cost of the Deluxe 4GH Plan is comparable to the Economy 4GH Plan.

There is a little knowledge you need to set up multiple websites on one account but that will be provided later.

Linux vs. Windows?

You should also understand you have the choice of setting up your hosting account in either Linux or Windows.

Expression Web will upload websites to either one, but depending on your need for databases and other applications, you might prefer one operating system over the other. However, there are differences between them. One key difference is the Windows operating system does not allow certain third-party applications to run on it such as Word Press and Drupal, but there are alternatives to these applications. The Windows operating system also runs ASP.Net and comes with two SQL Server databases. The Linux system does not. You should also note on the Windows operating system you can use Front Page Extensions, but cannot use PHP *and* Front Page Extensions. You must choose one or the other.

If you are committed to learning Expression Web, then you might want to go with the Windows operating system because you will have access to the .NET technologies and access to a couple of Microsoft Server SQL databases. You will also have access to Front Page Extensions but must give up PHP if you do that.

The main point is to be aware there are differences between Windows and Linux, and you will have to make compromises. If you choose one and later decide the other is better, you can switch but have to contact Go Daddy for assistance and might lose data in the process, especially if you have databases.

Once you have at least one domain name and have purchased a hosting account, Go Daddy will require you to set up and initialize it. You will do this through the My Products section on your My Account page.

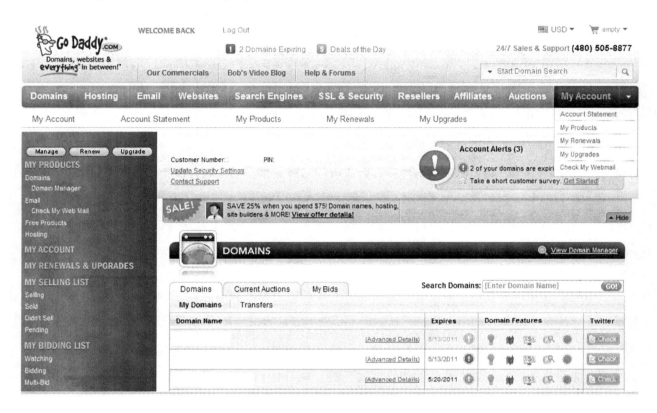

When you set up the account, one of the steps will be to select the domain name or domain names you want to associate with the account. If you only have one domain name, then you'll need to select that. If you have more than one, then select the names you want. If you need any assistance with setting up your hosting account, you can go to the Help Section or call Go Daddy for any assistance.

For the purposes of this manual, we are assuming you have your domain name and have already set up the hosting account and are returning to Go Daddy to prepare your account for uploading.

Let's review the process now.

When you return to Go Daddy, this is their home page as of March 2011.

At this point, you should have already purchased a domain name and initialized your hosting account, so it is simply a question of logging into your account.

After you log in, go to "My Accounts" tab as pictured below and choose "My Products."

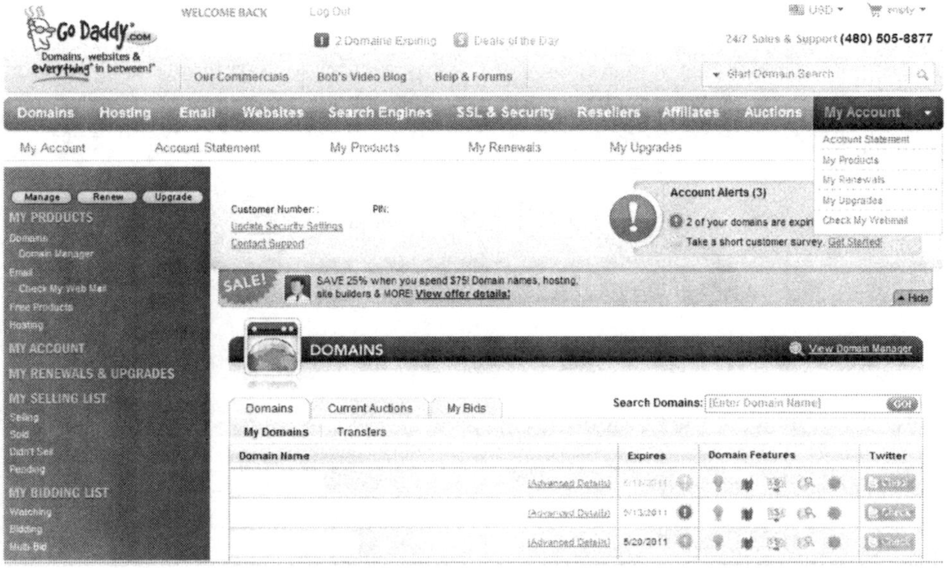

If you scroll down the page, you will see the heading that says, "Products" and under that, you should see where it says, "Web Hosting." Click on it, and you should see the following screen.

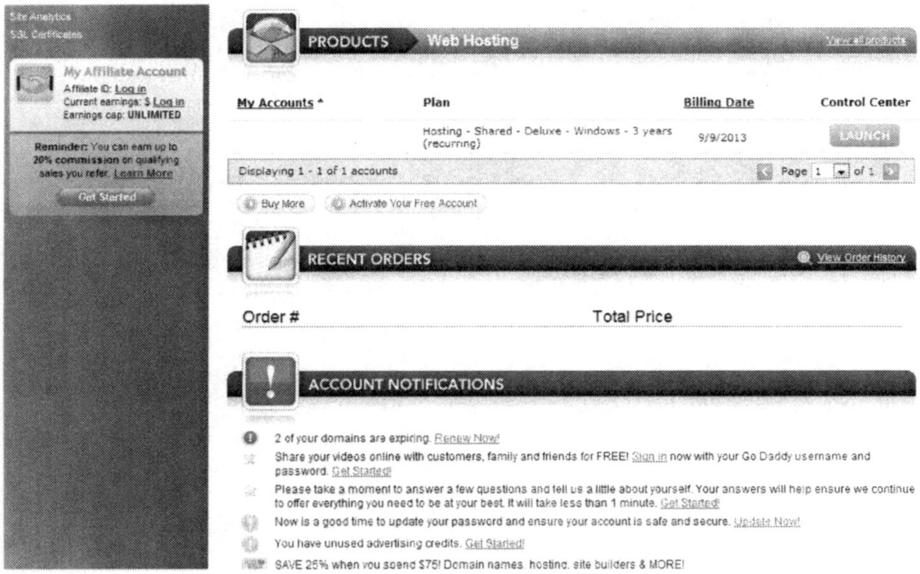

You can have more than one hosting account but if you have the Deluxe Plan, you shouldn't need more than one. Once you see your account, click the "LAUNCH" button pictured above.

The Hosting Control Center

The launch button will take you to the home Page of the Hosting Control Center, which as of March 2011, is version 2.11.0.

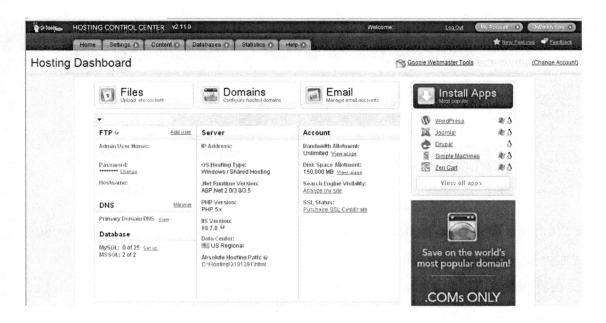

Let's briefly review this page.

You'll notice there are six tabs across the top of the page. These are Home, Settings, Content, Databases, Statistics, and Help. You should place your cursor over each tab to see what falls under each category. There is a lot going on here, so don't expect to understand what everything is or does. We will only be going over the minimum of what you need to know to upload your site. You can always go to the Help Section and research more on your own.

Beneath the six tabs, there are three large buttons: Files, Domains, and Email.

If you click the Files button, it will take you to the File Manager.

In order to successfully upload your site, you will need to have some knowledge of the File Manager. It essentially gives you access to any folders, files, and content you have uploaded to the hosting account and lets you do file management from within the Go Daddy site.

If you click the Your Domains button, it takes you to the Domain Management section where you can control all the directories, folders and files used in any website or application you upload. This is a very important area to understand if you are going to successfully upload websites. We have "doctored" the page a bit for purposes of illustration.

And last, the Email button transfers you back to your My Account page and lists all the email accounts you have up and running.

For the purposes of uploading a website, the only sections you need to know about are the File Manager under Files and Domain Management under Domains.

For purposes of illustration, we will be working through an actual Go Daddy account using the fictitious domain names *my.com* and *mybusiness.xyz*. (In reality, domain names must be at least three letters and there is no .xyz extension yet.)

Once your Hosting Account is set up, you go to the Hosting Control Center and click the Domains button. Once the page loads up, you should be able to see all the domains you assigned to your hosting account, and you will need to select the one you want as your *primary* domain. Your *primary* domain is important because it also serves your *root* directory and houses all the other folders and files you might upload. A star, as seen below, identifies which domain is primary.

Let's discuss this more.

You should remember a website can only have one home page or default.htm page, so once you upload a website to a host or server, the host automatically looks for the default.htm page in the root directory and will only display that page. The hosting account will only recognize one default.htm file per folder or directory. This is a key concept to understand—to be able to host multiple websites on a single hosting account, then the home pages or default.htm pages have to be in their own separate folders or directories.

Domain Management

Once you are on to the Domain Management page, click the Add Domain button in the upper right hand corner of the page.

This should pull up the "Add Domain" box.

```
Add Domain

┌─ Domain ──────────────────────────────────────────────────────────┐

   Adding a domain to this hosting account lets visitors access your content through a new URL. Deluxe and Premium plans can
   point an added domain to any new or existing subdirectory or nested subdirectory. To point this domain to the root ("\"), leave
   the default Folder setting. Economy plans can point to the root, only.


   Domain:            Folder:
   [              ]   [\          ]  [ Browse... ]




                                                          [ OK ]  Cancel
```

Now if you have already registered a domain name with Go Daddy, when you go to type it in the domain text field, it should automatically appear in a pop-up list.

If it doesn't, then usually the domain name is considered "in use" or otherwise unavailable. If this happens, you should contact Go Daddy Customer Service to find out what the issue is. It could mean a number of things, but usually it means the domain name is assigned to another product or server and needs to be reset. But don't spend too much time trying to figure it out. Just call Go Daddy and save yourself the detective time.

Sometimes the process of resetting a domain name can take up to 24 hours, but it doesn't usually take that long. Hopefully, this won't be an issue, but don't be surprised if it is. Many times the problem is something simple but something that was probably overlooked.

This is a good time to mention another good thing about Go Daddy and that is if you ever do have any question about how to do something, you can always call them, and they are available 24 hours a day.

Getting Help

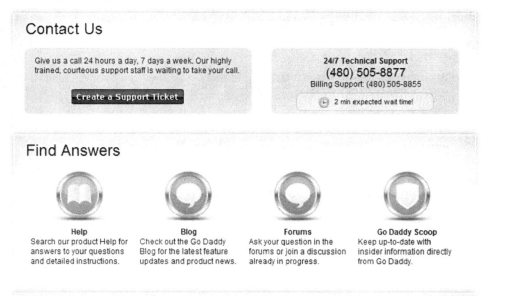

You might be placed on hold, but eventually you will reach a live person. We've actually called them at 3 o'clock in the morning to resolve an issue. They'll help you with some things up to a point but if it's related to something you are doing wrong on your computer or software, then they'll tell you there's nothing they can do; however, if it's related to something wrong with Go Daddy's systems, then they will, generally speaking, work through it with you. Be advised they are not perfect and like anything in life, sometimes it is hit and miss on the quality of information you get.

Creating A Folder For Uploading

Now let us return to the Add Domain box in the Domain Management section.

Your primary domain doesn't need a folder because it is loaded into one central location. However, if you will be uploading more than one website, then you have to create a folder (also known as a directory) in which to put all the folders and files for that site. If you don't make a separate folder, then all the folders and files will upload into the root directory, and you will have a giant mess on your hands because *two* default.htm files will be in the same root folder, and the remote server will only recognize one; therefore, only one of the sites will work or display on the Internet.

When the Add Domain box appears and you start typing the domain name in the Domain field, if the domain is registered with Go Daddy and available for use, the name should automatically appear in a pop-up list and populate in the "Domain" field.

Add Domain

Domain

Adding a domain to this hosting account lets visitors access your content through a new URL. Deluxe and Premium plans can point an added domain to any new or existing subdirectory or nested subdirectory. To point this domain to the root ("\"), leave the default Folder setting. Economy plans can point to the root, only.

Domain: Folder:

\   Browse...

OK   Cancel

Then under the Folder field, you must create a name on the Go Daddy server for where all of your website's files and folders will go. You can make up any name you want, but it should probably be something related to the name of your domain, so you will remember what it is. You will need to remember the name of the folder for when you go to upload the site to Go Daddy from Expression Web. Once you have entered a folder name, click OK. The domain should then appear on the Domain Management page and indicate it is pending set up by Go Daddy.

Understanding the "Folder" concept is very important if you are to successfully upload more than one site. What Go Daddy calls a "folder," Expression Web calls a "directory," so it can get confusing.

In short, for every domain and its associated website you want to host on your account, and you could, literally, host hundreds of them, you will need to create a folder for each one. So, if you had 100 websites you wanted to host, you would need 99 folders. And remember the primary domain would be excluded from this because it is in the root directory and doesn't need a folder.

When we upload the website from Expression Web to Go Daddy this should become clearer. It really isn't as intimidating or complicated as it might seem, but it is important to understand.

For our example, we are pretending we have two websites on our hosting account. One is the primary domain, *my.com*, and the other is *mybusiness.xyz*.

Now notice that while we don't have a folder (aka "a directory") for *my.com*, we do have one for *mybusiness.xyz*. We don't have a folder for *my.com* because it is the root directory, and it already has its own folder. However, for *mybusiness.xyz and* any other site we were to upload to Go Daddy, we would need to create and name a separate folder for each one. If we didn't, then all the files and folders for the website would go in the root directory and essentially be lost among all the files and folders for *my.com*.

Setting Permissions

We have one more thing to do and that is to make sure the Permissions are properly set on your hosting account. If they aren't, then even though you have created folders in which to put everything, you will not be able to write to them or post content in the folders!

To check and/or set the permissions on your hosting account, you need to go to the File Manager. To get there from the Domain Management page, click the Home tab in the upper left hand portion of the page.

Next we click the Files button on the Hosting Dashboard.

This will take you to the File Manager. In the File Manager, you should be able to see the folder you created and check or set the permissions to that folder.

If you click the box next to any folder the Permisson icon should light up on the menu bar.

Click on the Permissions folder and verify if the read and write permissions are set.

Set Permissions

Advanced Permissions

Set permissions for selected folders.

[✓] Read   *(Directory contents are visible to users)*

[✓] Write   *(Applications can write to this directory)*

[ ] Reset all children to inherit   *(All subdirectories will be reset to inherit from current directory)*

OK   Cancel

59 Directories and Files (1 Selected)	Refresh List		Page Size: 25	Page 1 of 3	
✔	**Filename** ▲	**Size**	**Date Modified**	**File Type**	**Permissions**
✓	[Root]			Directory	
	_derived	--	7/26/2009 10:27 AM	Directory	
	blog	--	11/3/2010 11:50 PM	Directory	
	blog1	--	7/16/2010 12:52 AM	Directory	

If they aren't, make sure those permissions are set and click OK.

If your permissions are not set, then it can block access to the folder you just created. Hopefully, all this will become clearer once you try your hand at creating your hosting account and start uploading sites yourself. But it can be a lot to take in, and it's easy to get confused and frustrated, especially in the beginning.

We have covered a lot, so let's do a quick review of the process.

Once you sign up for your hosting account, you'll pick a primary domain name. You can always change the primary domain later under Domain Management in the Hosting Control Center.

If you want to set up a new website to upload, you use the Add Domain function on the Domain Management page. When you add a domain, you have to create a folder for it separately from all the other folders on your hosting account. You can verify the folder has been created by going to the File Manager and seeing if it is there. Once you see it, check the Permissions to be sure it has read and write capabilities. Let's go back to Expression Web now and upload a site!

Uploading A Website

Open up Expression Web, go to the main menu, click File, then Open Site...
(If you have Expression 3 or 4, you can skip to page 112.)

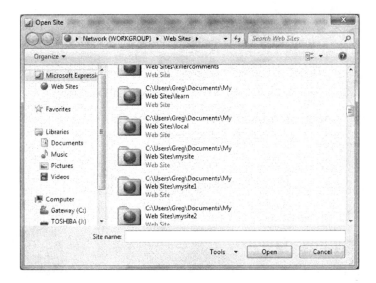

We should be able to find the website we were working on, which was titled "mysite."

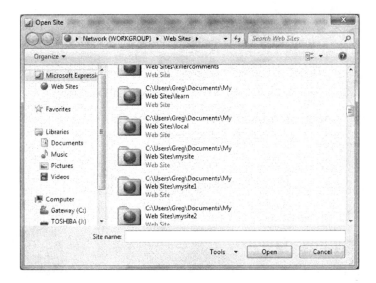

Now highlight the Website titled "mysite" and click Open, and the website should open
in Expression Web.

Once the site is open in Expression Web, make sure you are in website view by clicking the Web Site tab. If you are not on the Web Site view, you will not be able to upload the site. You will know you *are not* in Web Site view if you see the choices for Design, Split, or Code view on the bottom of the screen.

Once you are in Web Site view, click the tab near the bottom of the main screen where it says "Remote Website." These choices are only available in Website view.

Once you are in Remote Website mode, click the tab on top, "Remote Web Site Properties…"

And once you do that, it should open the Remote Web Site Properties dialogue box.

Make sure the radio button is clicked next to the "Remote Web server type" that says "FTP."

Now here is the important part.

In the field,"Remote Website location," type in the name of the "primary" domain.

In our example, the *primary* domain was *my.com*, so that is the name we would type in. You always type in the name of the primary domain because that is the root directory, so all the websites you upload will exist as folders *inside* or as subfolders of the root directory. You would type the name in as follows:

ftp://my.com

No need for www or a back slash.

Next, in the field that reads "FTP directory," this is where you type in the name of the folder you created on Go Daddy to house the website. In our case, we named the folder "business," so that is the name we would type in that field. There is no need to add slashes. Enter the name as illustrated below. Please note the vertical line after *business* is the cursor, not any kind of entry.

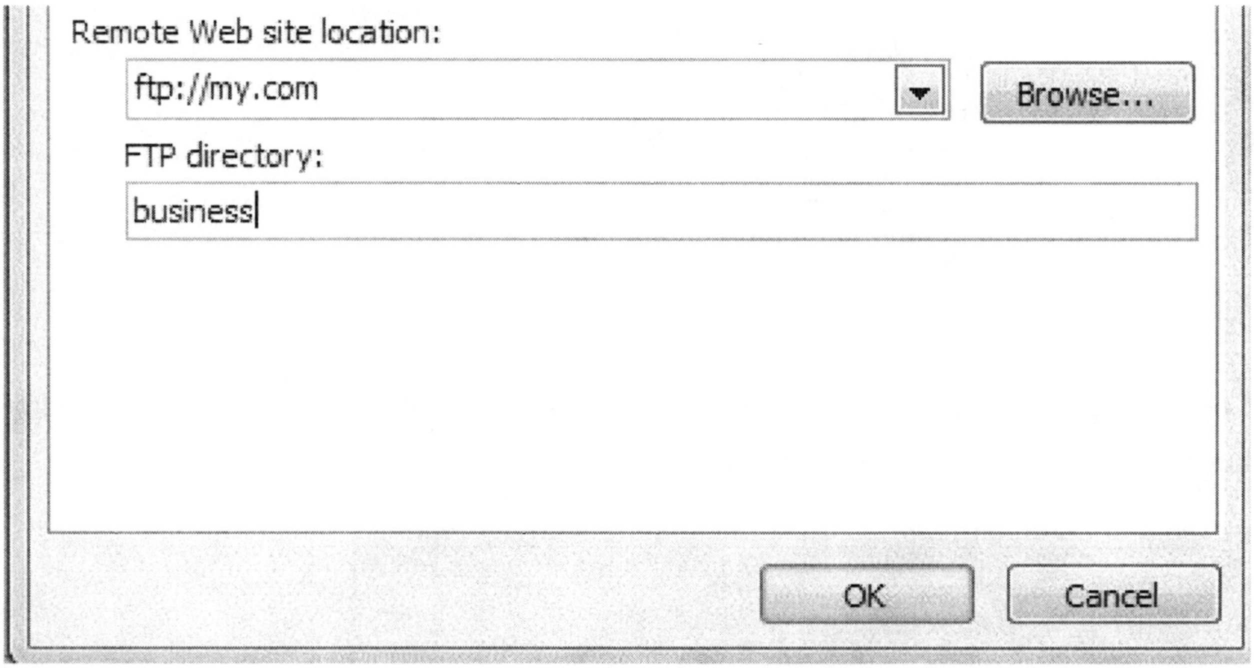

Remote Web site location:

    ftp://my.com   ▼   Browse...

FTP directory:

    business|

                              OK   Cancel

Also note that while Expression Web is referring to it as an "FTP directory," it is the name of the folder you created on Go Daddy. Don't get thrown off or confused by the terminology. Folder and directory are often used interchangeably.

After you are done doing this, click OK and you should be prompted to enter your User name and Password. You would enter your "User Name" and "Password" from the Go Daddy account you created.

Now click OK.

If everything is correct, Expression Web should automatically connect to the Go Daddy hosting account, and you should see the following screen:

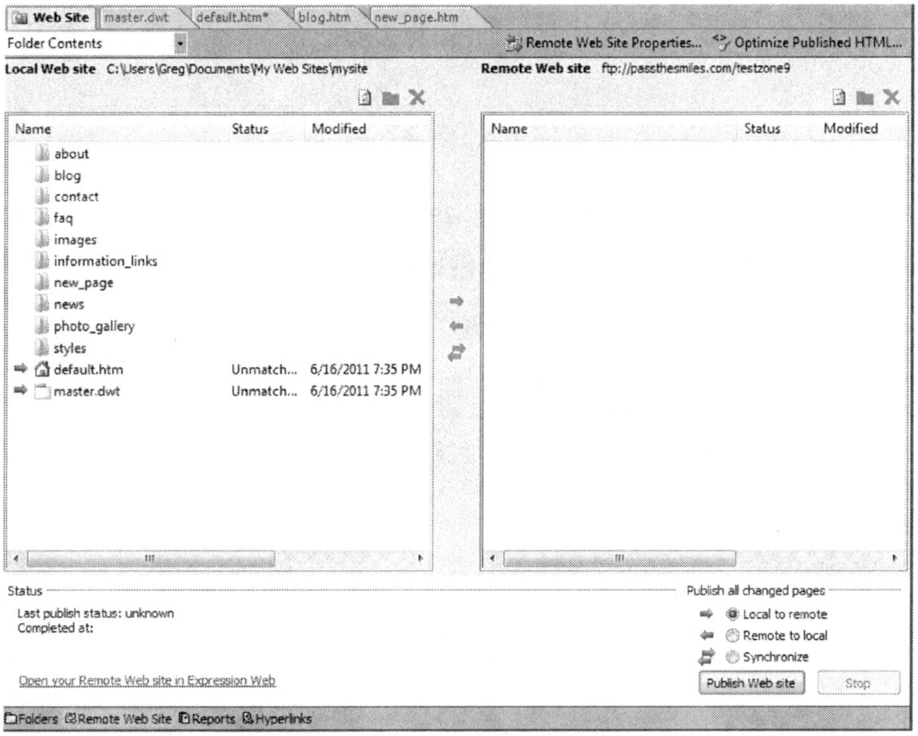

Let's take a minute to look at this screen.

On the left side is the "Local Web site" view. This shows you the folders and files for the website as they are stored on your computer.

Please note for the purposes of illustrating how all this works in reality, we are uploading these files from the actual C: drive on our computer to a real domain called "passthesmiles.com," which is currently on a Go Daddy hosting account. This is only because we have space available on that hosting account and are able to use the space to practice showing you how to upload a real site. If we were faithfully following our example though, we would be uploading to "my.com/business," not "passthesmiles.com/testzone9." The difference is *my.com* is an imaginary primary domain name whereas passthesmiles.com is an actual domain name with real space on a real Go Daddy server!

On the right side is the Remote Web Site, which shows you the storage area for the Go Daddy server or hosting account. It should be blank for the most part, though it might contain a Google file. You won't need that file for anything we're doing, so it can be deleted if you wish.

Now take special note of the "Publish all changed pages" section in the lower right corner of the screen.

Publish all changed pages ─────────────

➡ ⦿ Local to remote

⬅ ⚪ Remote to local

⇄ ⚪ Synchronize

[Publish Web site]   [Stop]

You'll notice it gives you three options: 1) Local to remote, 2) Remote to local and 3) Synchronize. If you ever want to download a website as a backup, you would create an empty website, then click "Remote to local," and click "Publish Website," which would download all the files and folders from the hosting account to your computer.

To upload a website from your computer to the hosting account, make sure the radio button is selected next to "Local to remote." If it is, all you have to do is click the Publish Web site button, and Expression Web will upload your website to the Go Daddy server. Click it now.

If everything went smoothly, your website should have uploaded, and all the folders and files that appear on the local website view should also appear on the remote website view.

| Web Site | master.dwt | default.htm | blog.htm | new_page.htm |

Folder Contents

Remote Web Site Properties... ⚙ Optimize Published HTML...

Local Web site C:\Users\Greg\Documents\My Web Sites\mysite

Remote Web site ftp://passthesmiles.com/testzone9

Name	Status	Modified
about		
blog		
contact		
faq		
images		
information_links		
new_page		
news		
photo_gallery		
styles		
default.htm	Unchang...	6/16/2011 7:48 PM
master.dwt	Unchang...	6/16/2011 7:35 PM

Name	Status	Modified
about		
blog		
contact		
faq		
images		
information_links		
new_page		
news		
photo_gallery		
styles		
default.htm	Unchang...	6/16/2011 10:4
master.dwt	Unchang...	6/16/2011 10:4

Status

Last publish status: successful

Publish all changed pages

Local to remote

If you see all the folders and files under the remote side, then congratulations are in order because you have just finished successfully building and uploading a website!

111

Uploading A Site Using Expression Web 3 And 4

If you are running Expression Web 3 or 4, the process is slightly different from Expression Web 1 and 2, so let's quickly run through the differences.

First, to open a website in Expression Web 3 or 4, you go to the Site tab on the main menu and choose "Open Site..." You don't go to the File tab.

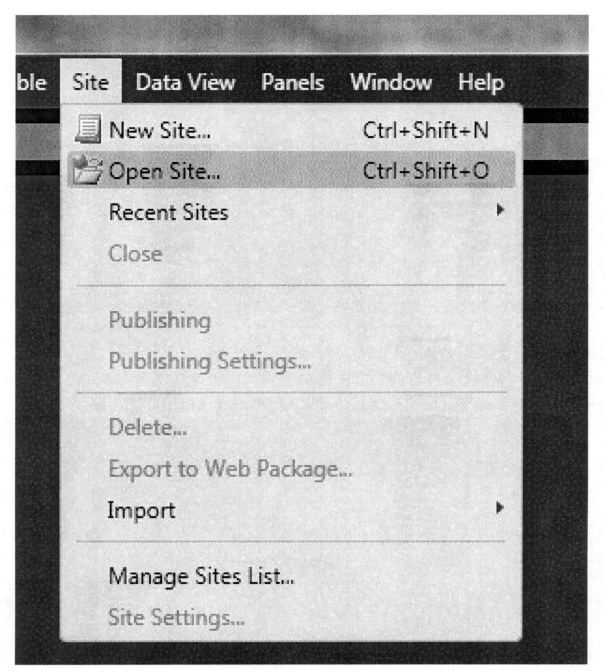

Second, in Expression Web 3 and 4, the Site View looks different. See below.

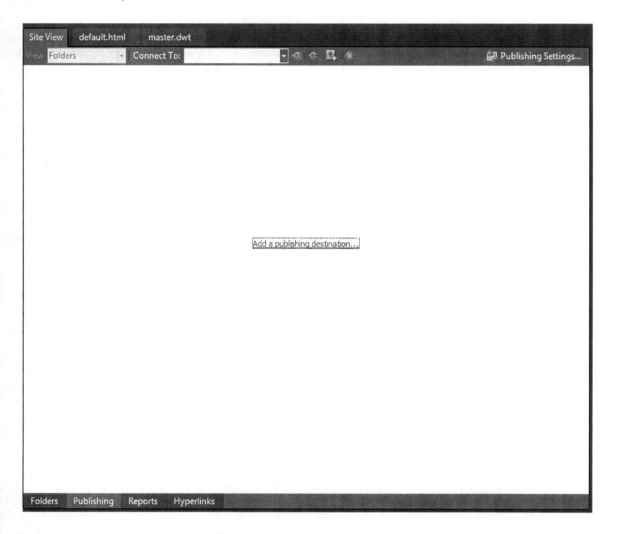

Instead of being called Website view, it is called Site View, and instead of being the Remote Website tab, it is called the Publishing tab. Also, it doesn't automatically give you a view of the local and remote websites, it presents a rather barren page view and leaves the next step sitting alone in the middle of the screen!

And third, to publish a website, click the link, "Add a publishing destination…"

Add a publishing destination…

Once you do that, this will bring up the Connection Settings box, which is a combination of two screens from the previous versions of Expression Web.

In this box, you type in a Name for your publishing destination. This name is for your reference only. Under the Location area, you type in the primary domain or root directory from the Go Daddy hosting account. In our example, this was *my.com*, and you type the name of the folder you created on Go Daddy to house the website's folders and files. In our example, the name of the folder was titled "business." You then enter your Go Daddy user name and password. You can leave the other settings as is, then click Add. It then returns to the barren screen with the next obvious choice just sitting in the middle of blank space.

Connect to the current publishing destination

And click the link "Connect to the current publishing destination." Note the "Connect To" drop-down box on the top of the page. This reveals the name of what the current publishing destination is. If you have other destinations, then you can switch to them from that box.

Once you click the link, it should automatically connect you to the local and remote views as shown below. From here, you click the top arrow to upload the site.

SECTION 6
PREPARING AND SUBMITTING TO SEARCH ENGINES

We are now coming to the final sections of the training. If you've been following along so far, you should have created a website by now and have it uploaded to a hosting account somewhere. However, we didn't completely finish the website because we didn't fully explain how to title the pages, add key words, or register it with any search engines. Without key words on the pages and without registering the site with the search engines, nobody's going to able to find your site. In this section, we will talk about key words and how to add them to your pages. We will also explain how to title your pages as well. And finally, we will explain how to register your site with three major search engines (Google, Yahoo, and Bing).

Self-Promotion

To get started, there are a number of websites that provide information on how to get your site on the Internet and appropriately indexed with the search engines; however, one site that seems to be a step above the others and provides a lot of good detailed information is selfpromotion.com.

Most of the information on this site is free and Robert Woodhead, the site's creator, does an excellent job of explaining how to come up with appropriate titles, key phrases, and content to get your site recognized by the search engines. He has one tutorial, in particular, titled "Preparing your Pages for the Search Engines," where he explains all you need to know to get going. You will find the article in the gray column on the right side of the home page under *Navigate / Tutorials*. He also offers additional services in exchange for modest donations.

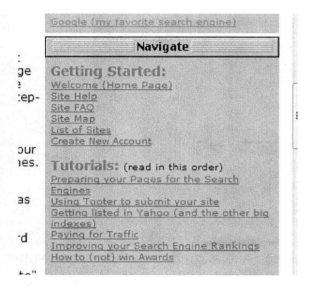

Setting Page Properties

Once you have read the tutorial and developed your key phrases and titles, then open your website in Expression Web.

The first step is to go to your home page, which is the default.htm page.

If you are in Code or Split view, switch to the Design view for now.

Once you're on your home page and in the Design view, right click your mouse and bring up the Page Properties window.

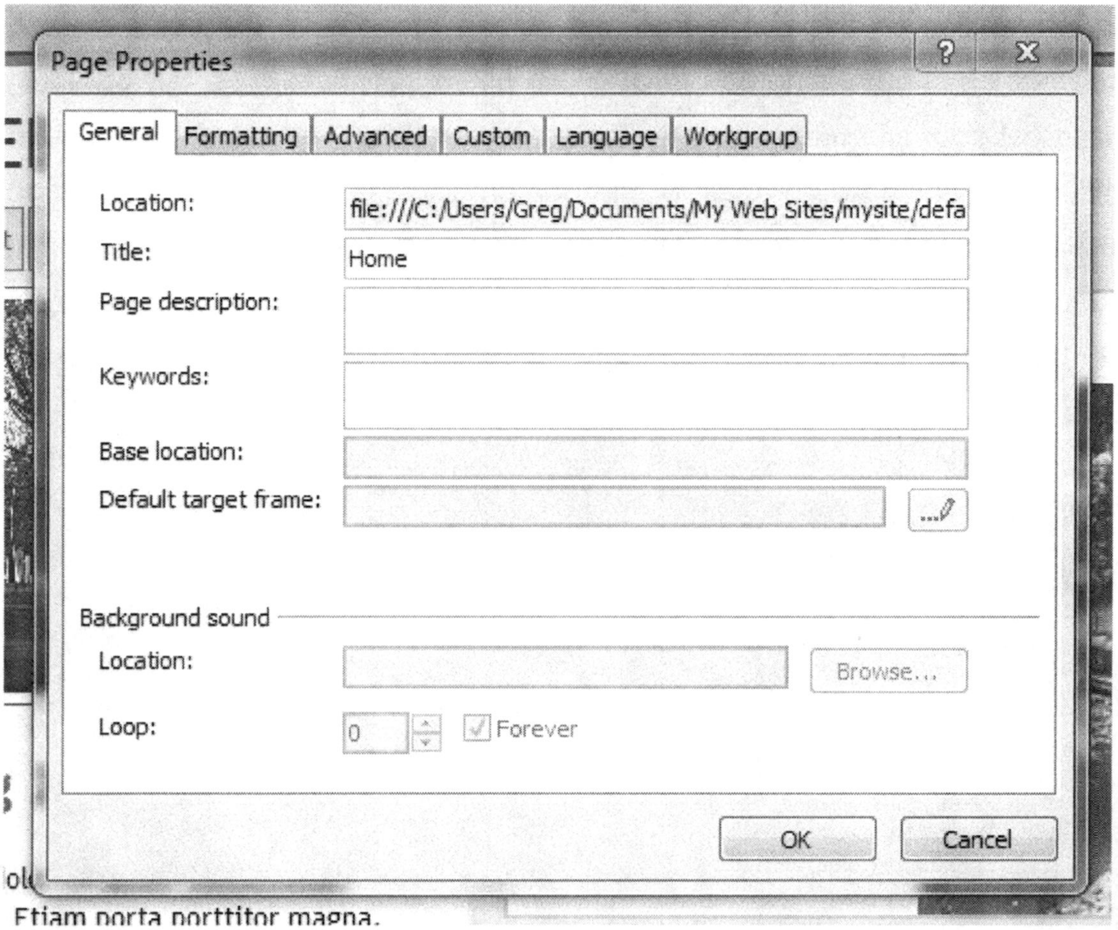

Page Properties dialog box — General tab

| General | Formatting | Advanced | Custom | Language | Workgroup |

Location: `file:///C:/Users/Greg/Documents/My Web Sites/mysite/defa`

Title: Home

Page description:

Keywords:

Base location:

Default target frame:

Background sound

Location:

Browse...

Loop: 0 ☑ Forever

OK   Cancel

Etiam porta porttitor magna.

Although we are starting with the home page, you will have to go through every page on your site and do the process that is about to be explained. And unfortunately, the content will be different on each page.

Now working from the Page Properties box, you will need to enter a Title, a Page Description, and Keywords in the corresponding fields. You should already have these in mind before you begin this process.

Since this is the home page, more than likely, the Title Field would include something related to the name and purpose of the site. The Page Description would elaborate on that, and the keywords or phrases would provide additional terms people might be searching for.

After all the information is entered in those three fields, click OK.

118

Now switch back to Code view and scroll up to the top of the page. You should see something that looks like this:

```
5
6  <head>
7  <meta http-equiv="Content-Type" content="text/html; charset=utf-8" />
8  <!-- #BeginEditable "doctitle" -->
9  <title>Home</title>
10 <meta name="keywords" content="home page, expression web, my site, " />
11 <meta name="description" content="This is my home page description." />
12 <!-- #EndEditable -->
13 <link rel="stylesheet" type="text/css" title="CSS" href="styles/style2.css" media="screen" />
14 </head>
```

Based on the information you entered in the Page Properties box, Expression Web automatically embeds it in the header portion of your code, so that's where it ends up.

Once you've done this, you need to go to every page on your site and repeat this same process.

More than likely, you will probably spend more time coming up with key phrases than you will be entering the information in Expression Web. Once you have completed this process for all of your pages and re-uploaded the pages to the hosting account, you are officially done with the website!

Now the only remaining task is to register it with a couple of the major search engines, and you are finished.

We are not going to register with every single search engine, though some people recommend you do that. For our purposes, registering with three should be sufficient for now. We never recommend paying to have your site indexed on any kind of search engine.

The three main ones are Goggle, Yahoo, and Bing, so let's go through the process now.

Google

To register your site with Google, you first go to the Google home page.

Once there, click the link "About Google."

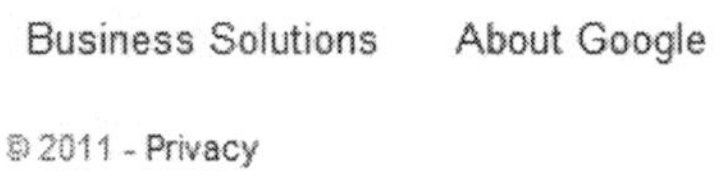

Business Solutions   About Google

© 2011 - Privacy

The following screen should come up.

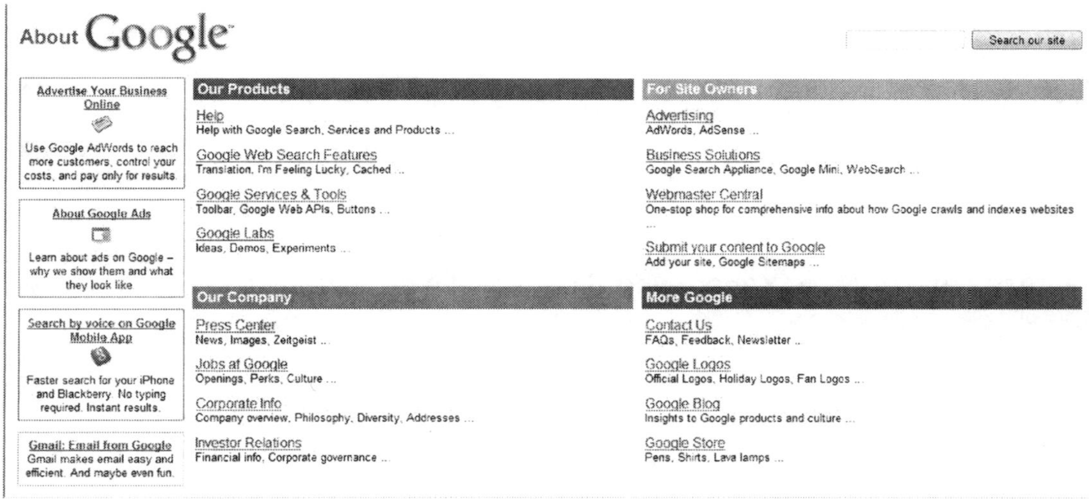

From here, go to the "For Site Owners" section and click the link "Submit your content to Google."

Then click the link "Submit a URL for inclusion in Google's index." This is located in the "Here's how to get started" box.

And finally you should end up on this page:

Once on this page, simply follow the instructions. Enter your full url or website address, enter the CAPTCHA word, and click, "Add URL." And that's it!

One warning: Do not submit your site more than once to Google. Once you submit it, if it is a good site and has good content, Google will probably index it. And sometimes, even if it isn't a good site, Google might still index it! But whatever you do, you don't want to make Google mad by resubmitting a site you already submitted. It doesn't make them work harder or faster. Unless you are paying Google to index your site by way of Ad

Words, Google has no obligation to list or index your site at all, so don't push it. If you keep submitting it, Google has the right to de-index and block your site, so relax, and it should eventually show up on their search engine.

Yahoo

Moving over to Yahoo, navigate to the Yahoo home page at yahoo.com.

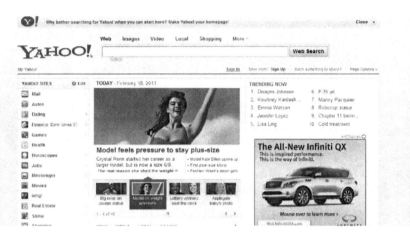

Once you are on their home page, click the link More directly above the Web Search bar. A drop-down menu should appear. Click All Search Services.

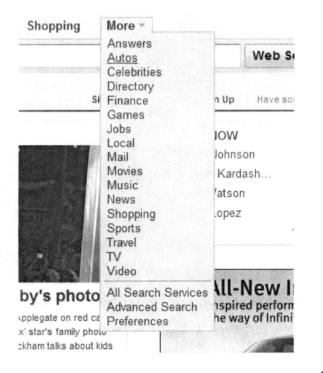

From here, scroll down to the Footer section and look for the link that says, "Submit Your Site." When you find it, click it.

Search Tools

Toolbar for Internet Explorer and Firefox

Search from anywhere on the Web and get one click access to your favorite sites—now available for Windows, Macintosh and Linux.

Shortcuts

Learn how to get the information you want faster with easy to remember search tips.

Enterprise Search Software

Download free, enterprise search software from IBM and Yahoo! that enables you to search your intranet, file systems, and the Web from one simple interface. It's free, easy to deploy, and easy to use.

Copyright ® 2011 Yahoo! All rights reserved. Privacy Policy - Copyright/IP Policy - Terms of Service - Submit Your Site

Once you are on the "Submit Your Site" page, click the link "Submit Your Site for Free."

YAHOO!® SEARCH _____ Yahoo! - Search Home - Help

Submit Your Site

The goal of Yahoo! Search is to discover and index all of the content available on the web to provide the best possible search experience to users. The Yahoo! Search index, which contains several billion web pages, is more than 99% populated through the free crawl process. Yahoo! also offers several ways for content providers to submit web pages and content directly to the Yahoo! Search index and the Yahoo! Directory:

Yahoo! Search Submission

Submit Your Site for Free:
- Suggest your site for inclusion in Yahoo! Search (requires registration).

Submit Your Mobile Site for Free:
- Suggest your xHTML, WML or cHTML site for inclusion in Yahoo! Search for mobile phones (requires registration).

And it should take you to this page that gives you a choice of submitting a website or feed.

Click on "Submit a Website or Webpage."

The link should expand and you should see this box.

From here, enter the full URL of your website and click "Submit URL."

Bing

You can also register with Bing, Microsoft's search engine, by navigating to this link:

http://www.bing.com/webmaster/SubmitSitePage.aspx

Once on the page, follow the instructions as shown below:

You are now registered with three major search engines. Congratulations! You made it!

We have covered a lot of ground since we first started and hopefully by now you have a general idea of how to build a website and what goes into the overall process. There is definitely a lot to learn, and you could spend a lifetime studying it all.

Our goal has to been to give you a general overview of the process and get you up and running on the Internet as quickly as possible. From here, you should keep learning as much as you can and slowly start customizing these templates to better meet your needs. You can experiment with changing the backgrounds, swapping out the navigation systems, adding graphics and logos, and adding interactive media. Eventually, the template will stop looking like a template and will start looking like your own original creation but that does take time and effort.

The next section is provided as a bonus and is considered optional for the purposes of this course. In the bonus section, we have information on how to customize the templates a little more.

SECTION 7 (BONUS)
TIPS FOR CUSTOMIZING YOUR TEMPLATE

Someone recently posted a comment on *learnexpressionweb*, our You Tube channel. The comment was posted after this person apparently watched the first series of videos on how to build a website using a template. The comment was:

"Thanks, this was exactly what I was looking for. Now the question is: How do I make a site that doesn't look like a template? LOL."

This is a good comment worth discussing.

When you get Expression Web and are starting to learn how to build websites, you have two choices. You can either build a website using a template, or you can try to build one from scratch. In our experience, building a site from scratch requires the highest degree of skill and knowledge so if you were starting out and tried to build a site from scratch, the result might not be all that great. That's not because you don't have the potential to be a fantastic website designer.

The problem is you don't have all the experience and skills you need to design the type of site you want. Building websites is a craft! It takes time to learn, and there is a lot to know to do it well.

All this leads us to the next option, which is to build a site using a template. And while it is true that a template site has a certain "template look" to it, a template site that a beginner makes will generally look better and perform better than a beginner's site built from scratch. We learned this the hard way!

Now here's the thing.

As your understanding of website building increases, you can begin swapping out and experimenting with modifying the templates. The templates are not carved in granite.

They were made to be customized and modified, so as your skills improve, you can begin the process of customizing the site to the point where no one will ever realize it was a template unless you tell them!

Every single element and style in a template can be changed or swapped out. You can change the background, the layout, the headers, the footers, and the total content. You can insert graphics and logos, completely new navigation systems, and add all kinds of interactive media and forms. The templates, in this sense, are really blank canvasses upon which you can design anything you want. But for the beginner, they serve as a stepping stone and entry point.

With this in mind, we would like to give you some tips on how to customize your template, so it doesn't look so much like a template and looks more like an original creation.

One of the most dramatic changes you can make to a template is to experiment with the style sheets. You can do this in many ways, but we will only be going over a few basics. In doing this, you will discover thousands of creative possibilities and no one way to do them. You can exercise control over the appearance of each and every pixel on the page and that's a lot of pixels. As you learn how to use Expression Web and how to work with HTML and CSS, you will slowly gain an appreciation of the artistry and craft that goes into the process.

Let's experiment with a style sheet now.

Experimenting With A Style Sheet

To do this exercise, go back into Expression Web and open the website we were working on. In reality, you can open any template you want, but for this example, we are staying with *Organization 1.*

You should have something that looks similar to the site below.

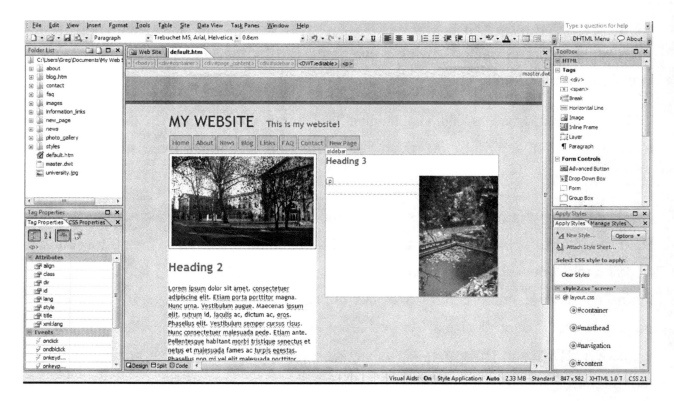

One of the key things to remember is the Style Sheet is controlling what goes where and how it looks. If you will remember from the section on Dynamic Web Templates (pages 78-79), you can go into the Code view on the master.dwt page to find which style sheet is controlling the look and layout of the page. Do that now for this site, that is, open the master.dwt page and find out which style sheet it is linking to, then open that Style Sheet in the main work area by double clicking it in the Folder List.

In our case, we are linking to Style Sheet 2. Your sheet should look something like ours.

Now take a moment to study this page.

First, we can see the style sheet is conveying a lot of information about how the site should look. You should take your time in looking the CSS code over and seeing how the CSS code affects the look and layout of the page. For instance, we can see the body section contains seven instructions. Let's take a closer look.

```
 1  @import url("layout.css");
 2  body {
 3      font-family: "Trebuchet MS", Arial, Helvetica, sans-serif;
 4      font-size: 0.8em;
 5      background-attachment: scroll;
 6      background-color: #90b7f1;
 7      background-image: url("../images/background.gif");
 8      background-position: top left;
 9      background-repeat: repeat-x;
10  }
```

You should know the body tags generally provide global instructions for the website and as such, they typically control the fonts and background imagery for the entire site.

```
 1 @import url("layout.css");
 2 body {
 3     font-family: "Trebuchet MS", Arial, Helvetica, sans-serif;
 4     font-size: 0.8em;
 5     background-attachment: scroll;
 6     background-color: #90b7f1;
 7     background-image: url("../images/background.gif");
 8     background-position: top left;
 9     background-repeat: repeat-x;
10 }
```

In the case of the template we are using, *Organization 1*, the body tag is being used to set the font type and size for the site. It is also being used to set the background imagery. This is more sophisticated than it might seem. For the top of the pages in the *Organization 1* site, the following CSS code:

background-image: url("../images/background.gif');

background-position: top left;

background-repeat: repeat-x;

…is instructing the web pages to repeat the "background.gif," across the top of the page from the left to the right. What is the background .gif? And where is it found?

The *background.gif* is a small image file, and it can be found in the images folder on the Folder List. Click on the images folder to see it.

When you double-click the background.gif, Expression Web will open the Paint program, and you will see the small .gif image displayed.

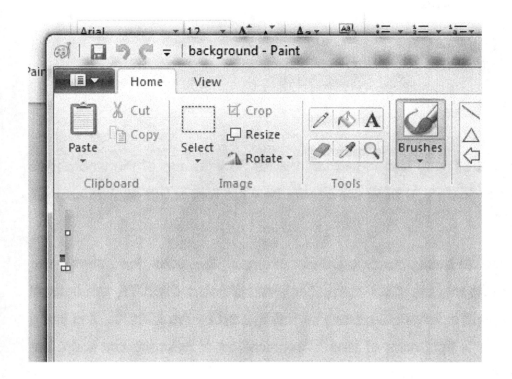

You can see what a tiny image it is but when it is instructed to repeat itself across the top of the page, it looks like a continuous block of colors; however, in reality, it is a single image repeated across the page.

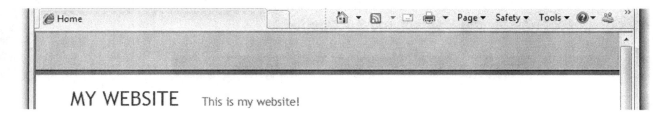

If you wanted to change that .gif file to another .gif or any other image file, it wouldn't be too difficult. And if you were to switch out the image, it would dramatically alter the appearance of the template.

Now let's return to our CSS code for a moment.

```
1  @import url("layout.css");
2  body {
3      font-family: "Trebuchet MS", Arial, Helvetica, sans-serif;
4      font-size: 0.8em;
5      background-attachment: scroll;
6      background-color: #90b7f1;
7      background-image: url("../images/background.gif");
8      background-position: top left;
9      background-repeat: repeat-x;
10 }
```

Since the CSS code has already issued instructions for how the top of the web pages will look, which line of code do you think will control how the rest of the background will appear?

For the rest of the available background space (for example, the sides, the bottom, and everywhere else in-between), the CSS code, *background-color: #90b7f1*, will instruct the web pages to be a light color of blue. Don't be intimidated by the #90b7f1. It is just a shorthand way of saying "a light color of blue." Technically, it is hexadecimal code, but we don't need to worry about that here.

The way the Organization 1 template is laid out with a width of 100%, you can't see any side margins, so you won't see the background on the sides. But if you preview the website by pressing F12, you can see the bottom background blue revealed on a couple of pages, most notably the Contact and FAQ pages.

After having walked you through this small section of CSS code, we hope you are starting to appreciate the relationship between the CSS code and the appearance and style of the site. There is a one-to-one relationship between what the CSS code is saying and what the pixels are doing. The pixels, in a way, are mindless soldiers who are only following orders from the CSS high command. Once you realize this connection, all you need to do is experiment with changing the code in the CSS file, and you will be able to radically change the appearance of your website.

Let's go through that now.

To do this, go back to the master.dwt file in the *Organization 1* template.

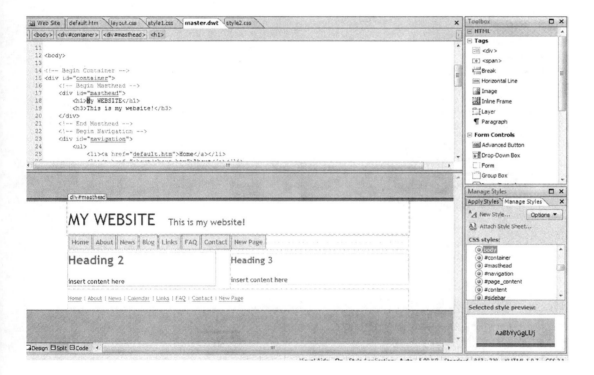

Now click the Manage Styles tab in the Manage Styles panel (lower right) and click the CSS styles until you get to the body tag that reveals the background.gif in the "Selected style preview" window. Be aware there are two body styles in the list, but we only want the one that controls the background.gif. Once you have found the correct body tag in the CSS styles window, right click it. A pop-up box will appear.

Choose "Modify Style…."

After you do that, the Modify Styles box will appear.

From within this box, you can easily alter the CSS code on your page and dramatically alter the appearance of your pages. Through the Modify Style box, you will find that it is simple to change the code on your CSS files and experiment with all kinds of changes and alterations.

Let's try a couple for fun.

Let's point out a couple of things first.

Under the Category box, if a category title is in **bold** as are Font and Background, then that means there are active instructions for that category with regard to the body tags. If the category is not bolded, then it means that category is not giving any instructions and isn't affecting anything related to the body tags.

The second thing is to be aware of the Preview window. It shows you what effect the CSS code is having on the appearance of things. As you change instructions and experiment, you can see them in the Preview and don't have to keep them if you don't like them. You don't have to save them all the way to the website and then preview the website. You can immediately see the effect of what you are changing.

135

For our experiment, we are only going to change two settings.

First, let's swap out the background.gif with a .jpg photo file and see what effect that has. Then, we will change the background color and see if we like it. After that, you can continue experimenting on your own.

To swap out the .gif file, simply click the Browse button and look for any photo you can find on your hard drive. Once you get to the photo, click Open, but do not click OK just yet. You should see a portion of your picture appear in the Preview window. In our case, we found a picture of a koala bear. Don't click OK yet!

Next to where it says "background-color," double-click the tiny colored box to the right of #90b7f1.

The More Colors box will appear as shown on the next page.

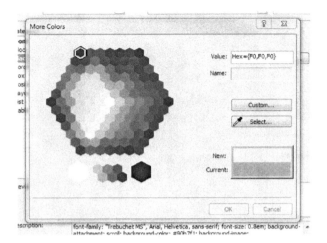

When it does, click the Select button and your mouse pointer will turn into a dropper. Once that happens, drag the dropper to anywhere on the screen where you see a color you think might look good on the website. You will notice that as you drag the dropper around the screen, the color in the New / Current box also changes accordingly. Once you have a color you like, click OK on the More Colors box and then click OK on the Modify Style box.

Now click Save and/or Save All. The "Save Embedded Files" box should appear.

Click OK.

Now go to the default.htm page and press F12 to preview the site.

This is what we got on the home page. You can see the top portion of the picture across the screen, but the rest of the background is blocked by the container.

Now let's go to the Contact page. You can see the image on the top and the bottom because the container is not as big as the one on the home page and is letting the background be seen. Since we chose such a massive image (10" x 8"), there is no available space for a background color to show through.

When we went back and cropped the image to a much smaller size and imported it again, the contact page looked like this and let the bottom background color reveal itself.

Experimenting with the style sheets is a great way to learn how everything works. And that is how you learn—by taking a chance, jumping in, and making your mistakes. It is all trial and error in equal measure and, in our opinion, that's the only way to really learn. There is no substitute for trying.

And for now, keep with it. You can master all this. It just requires time and practice! But most of all, whatever you do, be sure to have fun and enjoy yourself. Creating websites is both an art and a craft. It is a valuable skill to have now and for the foreseeable future. And for the current price of Expression Web, it is nearly impossible to go wrong.

We hope you have enjoyed these lessons and will email us or visit us online at expressionweb.us and let us know how you're progressing.

Leeds City College
Technology Campus
Cookridge Street
Leeds LS2 8BL

CPSIA information can be obtained at www.ICGtesting.com
Printed in the USA
LVOW091720221012

303944LV00001B/25/P